100 GREAT COUNTRY WALKS

100 GREAT COUNTRY WALKS

BEAVER PUBLISHING LIMITED

in association with

Country
Walking
magazine

First published in Great Britain in 1995 by Boxtree Limited
under the title *Country Walking*

This edition produced in 1996 by Beaver Publishing Limited,
9 Orchard Green, Alderley Edge, Cheshire SK9 7DT

10 9 8 7 6 5 4 3 2 1

Printed and bound in Italy by New Interlitho Spa. for

Boxtree Limited
Broadwall House
21 Broadwall
London SE1 9PL

A CIP catalogue entry for this book is available from the British Library.

ISBN 1 85962 039 6

Front cover photograph by Julie Fryer
Photograph opposite title page by Brian Hibbert

FOREWORD BY IAN BOTHAM

When I was asked to contribute to this book, first of all I sat down to think long and hard about what I was going to say, and then I decided that I would go out for a walk. It is when I am walking that I usually find that I can think most clearly. As I walked along the lanes near my home it occurred to me that, many years ago, for the vast majority of people this was the only form of transport. Then after the advent of the motor car but before the days of TV, video and computer games, people went out for a walk for relaxation and pleasure. Many people I know still do this, while others jump into their car to travel the few yards to their local shop. Children express horror when expected to walk to school – or anywhere else for that matter! I know people who have managed to cut out walking almost entirely and, after parking their car in a closely adjoining garage, walk the few steps into their house only to collapse into an enfolding armchair to press buttons on remote controls in order to view others being active on a TV screen. There are times when I can be numbered among them, but . . .

Mention the name Ian Botham and, apart from the odd exploit on the cricket field (and off) during my first class career, it is walking that most probably springs to mind. Walking, that is, not over hill and down dale, but along endless miles of tarmac from John O'Groats to Land's End, Aberdeen to Ipswich, Land's End to Margate, Liverpool to Yeovil via Wales, Belfast to Dublin and more. The idea for these charity walks began during Easter 1983 in the Lake District. Kath, my wife, and I set off from the small village church of Martindale to walk some distance around Lake Ullswater. What breathtaking views we saw that clear, cold, sunny day! While enjoying the beauty of our surroundings we chatted about life and our good fortune at the time and, in between Kath's gasps for breath as we strode up a particularly steep slope, I made a statement that has made a tremendous difference to our lives: 'I am going to walk from Land's End to John O'Groats for Leukaemia Research.' Over the new few weeks this idea grew and, some eighteen months later, it became a reality. On 26 October 1985 I set off with a few friends from John O'Groats to arrive in Land's End thirty-five days and 912 miles later.

On our way to the start we travelled the same endless miles of road I was soon to be walking along and the chatter died away as I realised the scale of the task ahead. The walking was tough, day in day out, averaging some twenty-six miles per day, non stop. At times we walked in silence for what seemed like hours, struggling with shin soreness, backache, groin ache, the pain sometimes excrutiating, only to have the physiotherapist work on us at the end of the day in order to get us on the road the next morning. But as we walked along the roads we saw some wonderful countryside, and at the pace of 4.5 miles an hour, we could see our surroundings in great detail.

Not everyone is going to set out to walk these distances. The wonder of walking is that everyone can enjoy it at whatever age and degree of fitness. You simply fit the length, the time and the place to your own circumstances. In this country we are very lucky to have so many accessible places to walk. Many authorities have worked long and hard maintaining ancient rights of way and public access to some of our most beautiful countryside, and I know that a great number of people take advantage of this and in doing so, see so much more.

In my long cricketing career I have travelled to many wonderful countries and met some fascinating people, but my greatest delight is when I look out of a plane window down on to the countryside of England and see the vast expanse of green. What a welcome home.

I consider myself extremely lucky to live in one of the most beautiful parts of England, the Yorkshire Dales. We are just on the Durham border, some forty-five minutes from the Lake District, so the opportunities to get out and take in the countryside are vast. I did this with relish after I had major back surgery in 1986. My quest for fitness and to return to playing for England began with gentle walks around home, building up to walks of twenty or thirty miles. Tigger, my boxer dog, and I would escape to see and hear nature as we ambled along river banks, through woodland, across moors. I spent this time walking making plans, working out problems, arriving home several hours later more at peace with myself and the world in general.

Walking is an occupation requiring no frantic planning. It is enjoyable to walk with family and/or friends, or entirely by yourself. The countryside – whether lakeside, seaside or meadow – is there for all. It demands nothing from us but has so much to give. How good to walk and enjoy it at your own pace.

IAN BOTHAM
Yorkshire, 1995

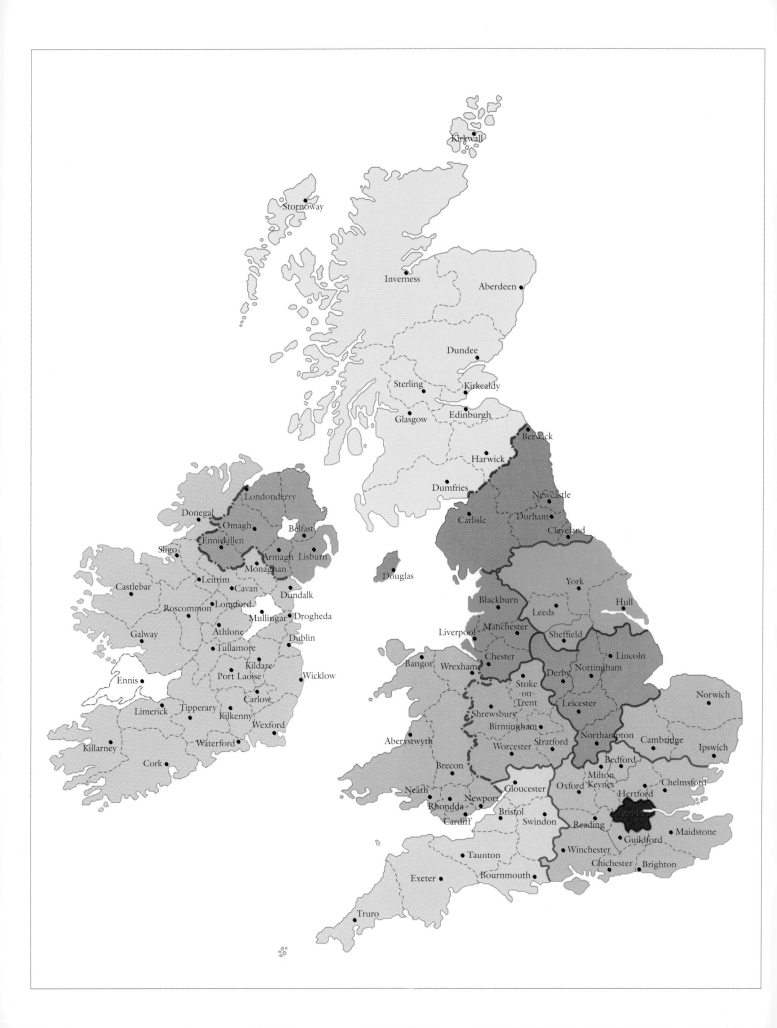

CONTENTS

EDITOR'S NOTE

The very first issue of *Country Walking* magazine in 1987 featured a selection of walking routes which we called 'Down Your Way'. Now, more than 2,000 walks later, it's likely that several of those routes have passed down your way; you may even have walked them.

The 'Down Your Way' pull-out guide has grown and developed to a point where it deserves a life of its own and, thanks to Boxtree Limited and Ian Botham, that is now possible. You are holding the result – one hundred popular walks chosen from Down Your Way over the last year.

If you're a regular reader of *Country Walking* magazine you will know what to expect – a selection of walks from all over the country, covering distances from five to fifteen miles, and suitable for a spread of walking abilities. Whether you enjoy striding out alone on coastal paths or exploring fells and valleys with your family, there's something for you in this book.

Along the way you'll discover the hidden corners of Britain, piece together bits of history, explore the ancient landscapes and be accompanied by the sight and sound of the wildlife which inhabits the beautiful British countryside. The routes are compiled by local experts with a wealth of walking experience and each walk is like having your own guide with you.

If you are new to walking or to 'Down Your Way', welcome to both. I hope you enjoy your first taste. There are some 11 million walkers and ramblers out there. Hopefully these walks will help you meet some of them while still being able to enjoy the peace of the countryside.

This beautiful book would earn its place on any coffee table but it's easy to use too. Browse through and plan your walks, using the area maps at the start of each section to help you.

The book is planned from north to south, starting with Scotland and taking in Wales and Ireland en route. Once you've found the area you want, use the index of place names at the back to pinpoint your exact location. These are based on the nearest towns to the walks.

Once you've chosen a walk check the fact file first. This will give you the distance, often including shorter or longer options, and an estimation of the time you should allow. It will also tell you a little about the terrain and the appropriateness of the walk for particular groups so that you can decide if it's suitable for you or your family. The stile information is especially useful for dog owners or older walkers. You will also find it useful to take the relevant Ordnance Survey or Harvey's map with you. And if you haven't got a car, don't worry. Most of the walks are accessible by public transport. Let this book be your first step to discovering some great walking country.

Lynne Maxwell
Editor, *Country Walking* Magazine

The symbols below are used for the route maps you will find with all of the walks.

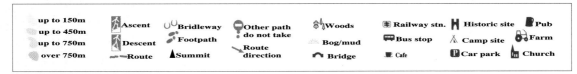

up to 150m	Ascent	Bridleway	Other path do not take	Woods	Railway stn.	Historic site	Pub
up to 450m		Footpath			Bus stop	Camp site	Farm
up to 750m	Descent		Route direction	Bog/mud		Car park	Church
over 750m	Route	Summit		Bridge	Cafe		

Facing page: Smardale Bridge in Cumbria. The Howgill Fells can be seen in the background.

Looking down on Glen Muick on the Balmoral Estate, south of Ballater – the popular route up to Lochnagar

SCOTLAND

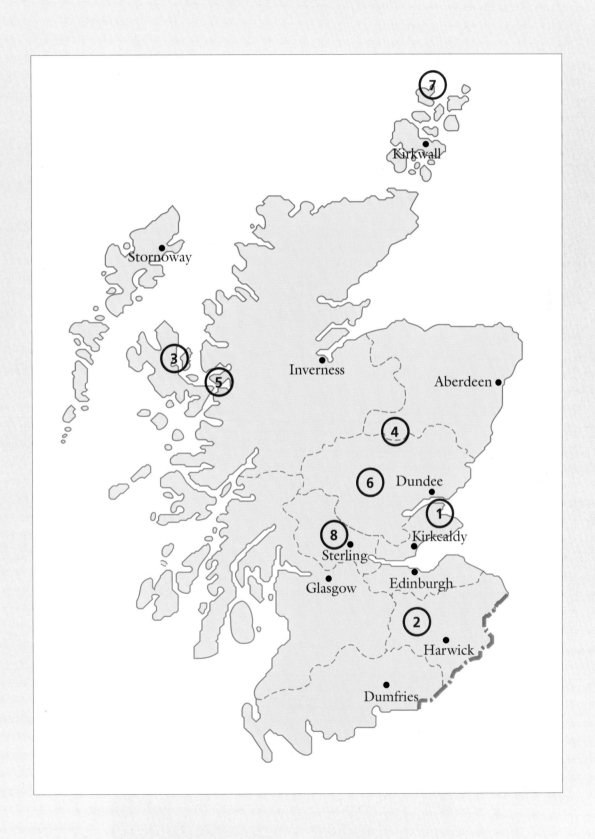

SAND AND SCOTS PINE

Rolling North Sea breakers crashing on to Tentsmuir Sands give way to the peace and tranquility of a woodland full of wildlife.

1 Set out from the Kinshaldy car park three miles from Leuchars and a wide path takes you out on to Tentsmuir Sands. Turn left and walk north over the wide expanse of beach. If the tide is out you may find it easier walking on the harder sand at the water's edge.

2 A mile on watch out for an old wartime look-out post up on the dunes. Close by there is a small concrete bunker set into the ground. Take a detour to the tower and enjoy the view from the top. There's a second outpost a little further on. Watch for grey seals and oyster-catchers on the sandbanks out to sea.

3 As you near Tentsmuir Point, 1 mile beyond the second tower climb onto the dunes, keeping the post and wire fence on your left. Stay with this to a point where it turns at right angles and runs west. Over by the tree line there are concrete blocks, a wartime effort to stop any invading tanks coming up the beach. On this walk you may also hear and see a more modern military presence: jets taking off from the RAF Leuchars.

4 Rather than following the beach around the point, where channels and pools of water are obstacles, it is worth cutting the corner and following the fence overland. Stay with the fence until you pick up the beach again.

5 Walk along the sand until you reach a row of concrete blocks at the top of the beach. To the left there is another corner in the fence and a low wooden stile. Don't cross this. To the right of the stile a narrow path runs into the forest and joins a more distinct one running parallel to the beach within the trees.

6 Meet up with a wide track on the left which curves up to the edge of the forest. Follow this west as it marches deep into the trees. In a few hundred yards an obvious track branches off to the left - don't take this.

7 Carry on until you reach the next track on the left and follow it south. There's a green post with the number 34 marked on it at the junction. The way stretches out in front through trees.

8 In 1 mile the track reaches a crossroads. Keep straight on here, crossing the Powrie Burn. The track eventually emerges onto the tarmac access road to Kinshaldy car park. Turn left and in a few yards you are back at the start.

FACT FILE

Distance 7 miles
Time 3 hours
Map OS Landranger 59
Start/parking Kinshaldy beach car park, grid ref 498243. Parking costs 50p
Terrain Level walking along sandy beach and on good forest tracks
Nearest towns Leuchars and St Andrews
Refreshments Cafe and pubs in Leuchars. St Michael's Inn, just outside Leuchars on Tay Bridge Road is a pleasant country pub
Public transport None
Stiles None
Suitable for Children and dogs. Swimming in the sea is not advised due to strong undercurrents. Do not venture too far out on to sand bars as they can quickly become cut off by the incoming tide.

The wide bank of sand dunes above the beach

ALONG THE WAY

Lying between the estuaries of the Tay and Eden rivers, Tentsmuir Forest covers 1,500 hectares and was acquired by the Forestry Commission in the 1920's. Planted predominantly with Scots and Corsican Pine, it is home to roe deer, red squirrels, butterflies and a variety of birdlife. Bat boxes have also encouraged Natterner's pipstrelle and brown long eared bats to roost.

REACH FOR THE HEIGHTS

Walk to Dunslair Heights, in the south-west corner of the Moorfoot Hills and visit the oldest Forest Enterprise property in the south of Scotland.

1 From the car park, walk north along Edinburgh Road to reach a house on the right, at the beginning of Venlaw High Road. Go through the access gate to the left of the large black gates and walk up the track ahead. After passing through a wooden gate you come to a second wooden access gate with a prominent path beyond. Don't go through this gate but cut up right on a narrower path, making for a metal gate ahead. Go through the gate and keep to the right of the grounds of Venlaw Castle Hotel. Walk up through an avenue of trees, to reach open ground to the left of newly planted woodland.

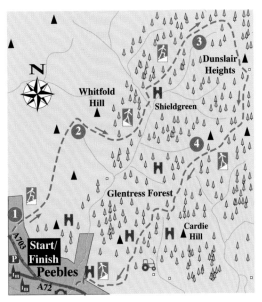

2 Follow the clear forest track uphill. After a short downhill section, the track makes a sharp right-hand bend and swings round the southern shoulder of Whitfold Hill. At the end of the track, bear left down a grassy path to reach a wooden gate that leads into more mature plantations. Walk down through the trees and at a junction turn left onto a main forest track. Almost immediately turn right, down a path leading to a wooden gate, with a sign 'Shieldgreen Centre'. Follow the path beyond to a footbridge over the Soonhope Burn. On the far bank, walk up to the large white house which is Shieldgreen Outdoor Centre.

3 Turn right, up the track leading to the centre, and follow a path up the left-hand side of outbuildings. The path goes up steeply behind Shieldgreen to a forest road. Cross the road and walk up through the trees to meet a second road. Follow the clear path beyond – this takes you up the open hillside to a saddle north-west of Dunslair Heights. Turn right at the saddle and walk up beside an old fence to the radio masts and meteorological station on the summit of Dunslair Heights. The views from the top are extensive.

The white building of Shieldgreen Outdoor Centre lies below Dunslair Heights

4 Leave the summit by a distinct forest road, heading south. Where the track swings right towards a fence, keep left, and follow a path through grass, with a broken wall on the left and the forest edge on the right. Soon cross through the wall, turn right, and continue with the broken wall on the right. Where a new wall starts, near a dark green marker post, turn right down a muddy track into the forest. At a main forest road turn left and walk downhill for just over 1 mile to a T-junction. Turn right and in 25yds reach another T-junction. Go straight ahead here on a footpath between trees. When you arrive at a clearing, follow the path round to the left to reach another forest road. Turn right and walk down the track for about 1 mile to a left-hand hairpin bend. A few paces beyond the bend, turn right on a steeply descending path to emerge onto the road opposite the goods entrance to Peebles Hydro Hotel. Turn left and walk down to the main road. Turn right along Innerleithen Road, then right into Edinburgh Road and the car park.

ALONG THE WAY

Glentress Forest lies among the Moorfoot Hills, which are to the north and north-east of the attractive, historical border town of Peebles. Covering an area of 2,817 acres, Glentress is the oldest Forest Enterprise forest in the south of Scotland, the earliest plantings dating from 1920. If you are visiting in the summer and time allows, drive south-east from Peebles to Traquair House. This impressive building claims to be the oldest continually inhabited house in Scotland. A total of 26 Scottish and English kings have sheltered here since the visit of Alexander I in 1107. Open May to September 1.30–5.30pm, July and August 10.30am–5.30pm. Tel 01896 830323.

FACT FILE

Distance 9 miles
Time 4½ hours
Map OS Landranger 73
Start/parking Peebles. Car park on Edinburgh Road, grid ref 254406
Terrain Clear paths and forest tracks throughout. A couple of short steep sections
Nearest town Peebles
Refreshments None on route. Facilities of all kinds in Peebles
Public transport – Regular bus service to Peebles from Edinburgh and other border towns
Stiles None. Several gates, please leave as found
Suitable for Older children.

ALONG THE RUGGED RIDGE

Climb Beinn Edra and enjoy spectacular views along the Trotternish Ridge, a giant landslip of beautiful scenery and geological wonders.

1 Start in the village of Uig. Set off up Glen Conon on the minor road which leaves the A856 on the north side of the road bridge over the River Conon, opposite a newsagent's. Initially the road climbs steeply over several sharp curves but eases off to rise more gently by some cottages.

2 The road undulates then ends by the last house. A muddy track strikes off ahead, passing over a low step stile. It runs over open moorland, which is used for sheep and cattle grazing. Ahead look out for spectacular waterfalls in a craggy little amphitheatre to the right.

3 After about 1 mile of good track walking, the way disintegrates into an indistinct path over a short marshy section. It soon reaches a fence running at right angles. Cross over and follow the fence down to the burn a few yards away, then pick up the path which runs up alongside the water. Ahead you can see the edge of the Trotternish Ridge. Aim straight for this point.

4 Follow the ridge up onto the summit, keeping close to a rusty fence. The climb is not particularly steep but great care should be taken not to tread too near the edge.

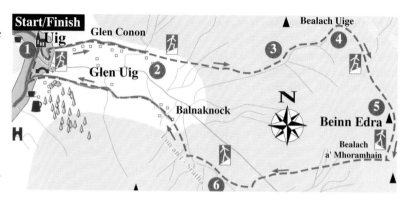

5 The summit is marked by a trig point, surrounded by a low circular shelter of stones. From here you can drink in the sheer spectacle of the Trotternish Ridge as it stretches south. There are also superb views west over Uig. Descend south then follow the path as it heads west on the return leg, dropping down into Glen Uig.

6 The path follows the Lon an t-Sratha burn down to the eastern terminus of a track and meets it by a croft at Balnaknock. The track soon becomes a minor road which leads back down into Uig, dropping steeply for the last few yards to the A856. Turn right at the main road and return to the start.

ALONG THE WAY

Stretching 20 miles north from Portree, the Trotternish peninsula has some of the finest scenery on Skye. It can be experienced first hand on this walk. The ascent, over gently sloping hillside, belies the true awe of the ridge which becomes apparent only when you are right up on the craggy borderline between east and west. The starting point, Uig, is one of the main ferry ports for the Outer Hebrides.

FACT FILE

Distance 7½ miles
Time 3–4 hours
Map OS Landranger 23
Start Junction of A856 and minor road up Glen Conon, Uig, grid ref 398639
Parking Small layby a short way from the start by junction of A855 to Staffin
Terrain Minor roads and path over open hillside
Nearest town Portree
Refreshments Uig
Public transport Skye–ways Kyleakin–Uig and Glasgow–Uig bus services, tel 01478 612075
Stiles One
Suitable for Children. Dogs should be on leads due to grazing. Care should be taken along the ridge as there is a steep drop to the east

The spectacular Trotternish Ridge provides excellent views

MIGHTY MORRONE

Climb the Corbett and enjoy views over Deeside and the Grampian mountains.

1 Set off from the public car park at the top of Chapel Brae, Braemar, heading west along a track. A short way on at a junction turn left and follow the track south up into the Morrone Birkwood Nature Reserve. Pass a house on the left and climb through birch and juniper to a viewpoint where a plaque identifies surrounding hills.

2 Nearby, a small cairn has information on the nature reserve and to the left of this there is a marker post with 'Morrone' etched on it. A path strikes out over open hillside, climbing to a deer fence. Rather than a gate or stile there is a wooden 'passageway' through the fence which deer can't negotiate. The ascent is hard work, rising to a line of cairns at an altitude of around 2,460ft.

3 The top is still a little way off but the cairns mark the start of a more gradual ascent. There are excellent views over Braemar to the mountains of the Cairngorms. As you gain height the heather thins out to reveal more stony ground and soon a large aerial mounted on the summit looms into view.

4 The top of Morrone stands at 2,815 ft. In addition to the trig point and a large cairn, the summit boasts a radio relay station. Continue the walk by descending south on a wide track dropping into Glen Clunie.

5 At the valley floor the track meets up with a minor tarmac road opposite Auchallater farm. Turn left and walk north, keeping an eye out for traffic. The road runs beside the Clunie Water towards Braemar Golf Club.

6 Just beyond the clubhouse on the left-hand-side of the road, there is a wooden marker post with a blue strip painted on it. Leave the road here, turn left and follow a path up towards several static caravans perched on the hillside. Behind them a stile crosses a fence and once over this you're back in woodland. The path is indistinct through the trees but you should head diagonally right up to the top where another wooden gateway passes through a deer fence.

7 The path skirts round woodland, bringing you back to the view-point. From here retrace your steps to the car park.

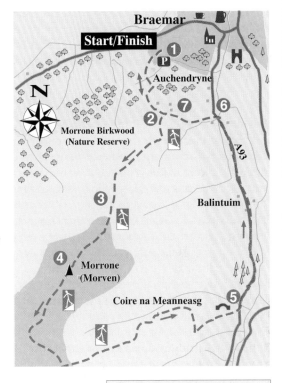

ALONG THE WAY

Morrone is classed as a Corbett – these are Scottish mountains between 2,500 and 2,999ft high with a drop of 500 ft on all sides. The list of 221 tops was drawn up by J. Rooke Corbett. The Morrone Birkwood Nature Reserve is described as one of the finest examples of upland birchwood in Britain. The trees line the lower slopes of Morrone. 'Morrone' itself translates from the Gaelic as 'big nose' which is a fair description of this prominent mountain.

Morrone looms up behind this weather hut in Braemar

FACTFILE

Distance 7 miles
Time 4 hours
Map OS Landranger 43
Start/parking Public car park at top of Chapel Brae, Braemar, grid ref 143911
Terrain Track and path through trees and over open hillside. About 1½ miles on minor road
Nearest town Braemar
Refreshments Plenty in Braemar
Public transport Bus service to Bramar from Aberdeen
Stiles Just one
Suitable for Fit walkers and older children. Braemar Golf Club requests dogs on leads through their course.

THUNDERING WATERS

A strenuous circuit where hard work is rewarded by the breathtaking Falls of Glomach which thunder dramatically down into a deep leafy gorge.

1 Follow the narrow tarmac road east from the National Trust for Kintail Countryside Centre, along the edge of a campsite. Pass an outdoor centre and then a B&B before crossing the River Croe on a susbstantial wooden and metal bridge.

2 Across the water a footpath heads straight over the grass, signed for the Falls of Glomach. Pass a couple of rope swings and the path turns right to cross a small wooden bridge. The path then becomes much more obvious but is a bit wet and muddy in places. After crossing open moorland it meets up with the river and runs alongside it for a distance before climbing gently up over the hillside. All around, narrow waterfalls cascade down over the steep slopes and some converge on the path, making it very wet underfoot for much of this stretch. Make sure your boots are waterproof.

3 After about 1 mile a green National Trust for Scotland sign points you left and you descend into the vegetation by the river. A path falls to the right and the way crosses on a footbridge. On the far side, climb out of this little wooded flen, go through a kissing gate and turn left. Follow a track down through another gate and carry on to a car park a little way ahead.

4 Another sign points up the track to the right. Once through a green barrier gate, there is a strenuous climb until the way levels off and runs through the forest.

5 The track narrows into a path, crosses the burn by a bridge and then climbs steeply up the hill. This continues for some way and then evens off before rising and falling up to the Bealach na Sroine. It's hard going but the views are excellent with many spectacular waterfalls crashing down into the valley below.

6 A line of cairns marks the way through the pass and then the descent begins, first gently then more steeply as you get nearer to the falls.

7 The Falls of Glomach are spectacular and make the lengthy walk worthwhile. You'll catch a glimpse of the bubbling broth from the top, but a narrow path descends a little way to a small viewpoint, curving round so the waterfall can be seen head on. Take great care here as it is a long way down. Keep children and dogs in check too, From the falls head up the bank of the Abhainn Gaorsaic. There is no obvious path but follow the river up into the glen and a series of small lochans.

8 From Loch Gaorsaic a path climbs up to the right. Follow this into Bealach an Sgairne then descend into the glen, taking care as it is steep and narrow in places. The path skirts round the hillside bringing you back onto the first part of the ascent. Retrace your steps to the Kintail Countryside Centre.

ALONG THE WAY

The Falls of Glomach are among the highest in the British Isles and include a sheer fall of around 300ft. They are on the Kintail and Morvich estate which was bought by the National Trust for Scotland in 1944.

FACT FILE

Distance 12 miles
Time 6 hours
Maps OS Landranger 33
Start Kintail Countryside Centre, Morvich, grid ref 960210
Terrain Forestry tracks and path over open moorland; very wet in places. One section over rough ground without path but route finding is easy.

Nearest town Kyle of Lochalsh
Parking Car park at Centre
Refreshments Cafe on A87 by southern access road to Morvich. Wide choice in Kyle of Lochalsh
Public transport None
Stiles None
Suitable for Older children and dogs, making sure they stay well back at the falls

ROUND THE LITTLE LOCH

Good tracks take you through moorland to Loch Ordie, a small lochan in the low hills north of Dunkeld and, on a warm day, a good spot for a paddle.

1 Arriving by car on the A9, take the Dowally turn-off that is prominently signposted for a craft centre and restaurant. A minor road takes you to the craft centre but park on the disused bridge or roadside verge at the end of the driveway. Set off across the bridge and up a Tarmac path which runs alongside the A9 for a short distance to Dowally, where there is a picturesque row of cottages and a church, St Anne's kirk.

2 Follow the narrow road up past the houses to a grassy track which curves right and then left and climbs fairly steeply up through a ribbon of mixed woodland. At the top a stile takes you out onto an open farm track.

3 Turn right along the track and then almost immediately turn left, passing through a kissing gate. Continue up this

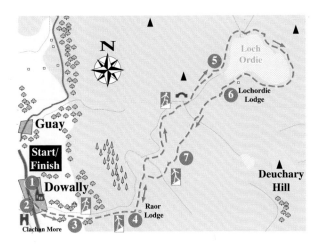

farm track which rises above the tree-lined burn down to the left and is bordered on the right by open fields. Depending on weather conditions, flies can be a nuisance here so it is worth taking a repellent or hat if they bother you.

4 Go through a gate and head left on the track which passes along the front of Raor Lodge, a farmhouse. This takes you out over heather-covered moorland and sheep grazing country, following close by the burn that runs down from Loch Ordie to the River Tay just below Dowally.

5 The loch remains hidden from view until you are just a few yards from the water's edge. The track heads off to the left and you can pick your way around the shore. On a calm day, watch out for fish jumping in the water. At the most northerly end of the loch, the track bears left. Cross a bridge to the right and follow a grassy path which runs around the loch and meets up with a track on the far side. This guides you to Lochordie Lodge, a row of three cottages which overlook the water and are used by fishermen.

6 At the right-hand end of the cottages, a path rises up on to the hillside, flattens out and runs over the heather round the western flank of Deuchary Hill.

7 After about 1 mile, a fairly distinct grassy path branches off to the right and descends through the heather to a gate which sits by a lone pine tree. The path continues across an open field, rejoining the track to Loch Ordie just north of Raor Lodge. From here, it is just a case of retracing your steps down to where you started in Dowally.

ALONG THE WAY

Although relatively low lying, the countryside of this part of Perthshire is impressive, dotted with beautiful little lochans and spectacularly craggy hillsides. As you round Loch Ordie, keep an eye open for the rocky outcrops below the summit of Deuchary Hill, and the birds of prey that make their home in such terrain. If you are quiet you may be lucky enough to spot deer on the open moorland.

FACT FILE

Distance 7 miles
Time 4 hours
Map OS Landranger 52 or 53
Start Dowally, grid ref 001482
Terrain Track and path
Nearest town Dunkeld
Parking Quiet roadside
Refreshments Wide choice in Dunkeld
Public transport None
Stiles Two
Suitable for All. Dogs on lead north of Raor Lodge as there are sheep grazing

The Knap of Howar dates back to 3600BC

NATURAL PARADISE

Explore the beautiful island of Papa Westray, rich in history and wildlife

1 From the ferry turn right through the gate at the pier head and follow the track turning north at the next gate. As you progress along the cliffs you will need to climb a low wall; watch out for the black guillemots at the same time. After the ruins of Blossom and Cuppin detour inland at grid ref **501509** to the ruined St Tredwell's Chapel on a promontory in the loch of the same name. St Tredwell tore out her own eyes and sent them to an admirer to cool his ardour.

2 Continue north past the ruins of Hookin Farm and Mill. In the 17th century oats were ground here. Watch for shore birds on the beach. After a wooden gate and Links Farm, join the tarmac road to the old pier.

3 Follow the track north, or walk along the beach, to the north of North Via. The first farm on the left is Skennist – from the old Norse 'skeidanaust', a place where large boats were hauled up for the winter. Pleasant wetlands lie to the left and watch out for seals and shorebirds on the right. You might come across tiny cowrie shells along the tideline too.

4 Walk north along the beach to Weelie's Taing – seals haul out here and birds come to bathe and feed. Early in the year there is a fresh water pool over the bank which is good for wildfowl. Weave your way northwards through the ruined sheep shelters and follow the sheep-track to the Fowl Craig with its breeding seabirds (but not after July). Look for the memorial to the Great Auk shot here in 1813 – it was the last in Britain. You are now on the North Hill Bird Reserve, the finest stretch of maritime heath in Britain. Please read the notice and keep near to the coast to avoid disturbing the Arctic terns and Arctic skuas. Behind the Fowl Craig there is a good area for the rare Scottish primrose, a tiny amethyst flower with a yellow centre. Walk right around the headland.

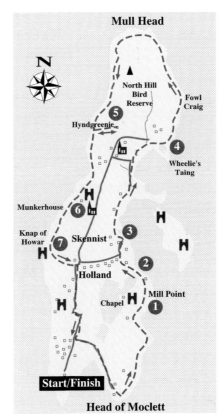

5 At Hyndgreenie, a white coastguard hut near the southern exit of the reserve, the RSPB has a small observation centre with useful information. The summer warden may be here or at Rose Cottage.

6 Return to the west coast and continue south to Munkerhoose. This name refers to massive stone remains in the cliff, all much eroded by the sea. The recently restored church of St Boniface probably dates back to the 8th century and stands on top of a 10 acre site from the 6th century. Take a look at the charming tile picture in the kirk created by the present primary school pupils and in the church-yard look for the pink sandstone 'hogback' Viking gravestone.

7 Continue south to the Knap of Howar, an ancient farmstead dating to 3,600 BC. Go south-west to the farm of Holland (high land), taking the tarmac road south to the links of Moclett with its flower-studded turf and the pier.

FACT FILE

Distance 8½ miles
Time 5 hours
Maps OS Landranger 5, OS Pathfinder 23.
Start Moclett pier, grid ref 495493. If you are staying on the island or arriving by air you could start at Holland Farm, grid ref 488516
Terrain Sheep tracks, quiet island roads, beaches and clifftops. Keep well away from all rocks sloping into the sea, there is no way back following

an accidental slip.
Nearest town Kirkwall
Refreshments Papay Community shop/guesthouse
Public transport Boats go to Papay from Kirkwall every day (on Sundays in summer only). British Airways flies there twice a day with eight-seat planes, but not Sunday. Further information form Orkney Tourist Board. Kirkwall, tel 01856 872856
Stiles None
Suitable for Children

NOTE This walk is not along a right of way, but the islanders welcome visitors. Please ensure continuing tolerance by observing the Country Code.

ALONG THE WAY

The northern Orkney island of Papa Westray – 'Papay' is 4 miles by 1 mile. It has the oldest standing house in north west Europe, a part 12th century church, an enormous breeding colony of Arctic Terns and on an adjoining island – the Holm – a tomb that is more than 5,000 years old. Seals glide alongside as you walk the fine sandy beaches. There are also wetlands, cliffs and heaths with the rare Scottish primrose.

ROB ROY TERRITORY

In the shelter of the vast Loch Ard Forest are quiet lochs, open areas
of farmland and extensive broad leaved woods.

1 Take the narrow road over the hump-back bridge which crosses the Forth – this quiet hill burn becomes the mighty river at Edinburgh. Continue past the old church and through the outskirts of the village.

2 At Balleich a Forestry Commission sign points left to the Doon Hill Fairy Trail. Take the right track. If you want to shorten the walk, you can start from here where there is limited parking. Continue on the main track, ignoring all turnings off.

3 After about 2 miles there are two branches to the right in quick succession. Take the second of these, a narrower, more overgrown track.

4 After a sharp right-hand bend go left at the T-junction.

5 Turn right. Ignore the next turning to the right and soon you will see Lime Hill beyond the next junction, rising above a little gorge on the Kelty Water. Climb carefully to the summit and pause to admire the views before returning to point 4. Continue straight past the junction this time.

6 Turn left at the next junction and, shortly after, go right onto the narrower track. This rises to an open area, which has a cairn at the summit and descends below an aqueduct.

7 Turn sharp right and keep going along the main track, ignoring all turnings off.

8 When you reach the Covenanters' Inn go left to return to Aberfoyle, or right to Balleich.

ALONG THE WAY

Much of Sir Walter Scott's *Rob Roy* is set in Aberfoyle. Notice the old church on the outskirts of the town. Robert Kirk, minister here in the late 17th century, wrote a book, *The Secret Commonwealth*, about his belief in the fairies. He also translated the Psalms into Gaelic.

In the forest watch out for the large domes of pine needles that mark the nests of wood ants.

The Loch Ard Forest provides beautiful scenery at every turn

FACT FILE

Distance 11 miles
Time 5–6 hours
Map OS Landranger 57. NB Loch Lomond Tourist Map doesn't show all forest tracks
Start/parking Aberfoyle, grid ref 522009
Terrain Good forestry paths and tracks. Lime Hill is a short, rough climb, easier in winter when the bracken is dead
Nearest town Aberfoyle
Refreshments Pubs, cafés, hotels, chip shop in Aberfoyle
Public transport Bus stop adjacent to tourist information centre at car park. Midland Bluebird service 11/211 links Aberfoyle with Stirling and Glasgow. In summer Aberfoyle is also served by Trossachs Trundler vintage tourist bus service. For information, tel 01786 442707
Suitable for Children. If the walk is too long, it can be shortened at various points. Particularly recommended after fresh snowfall

THE NORTH

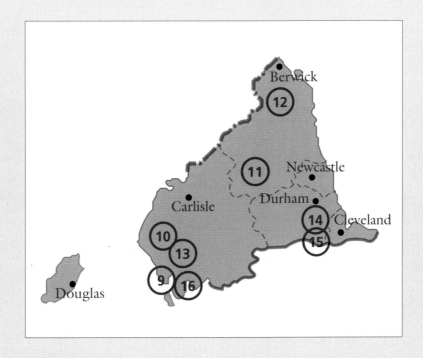

BLACK AND WHITE

This easy climb up Black Combe reveals a superb panorama, which Wordworth described as 'the amplest range of unobstructed prospects that British ground commands'.

1 Cars can be parked at Whicham church, though walkers can use BR services and start nearly a mile away at Silecroft station. A farm access road runs from Whicham church to Kirkbank, where a track climbs above the whitewashed farm to reach the fell gate. Beyond the gate you emerge onto open fellside where the climbing starts in earnest.

2 A broad, grassy path takes you uphill into a bracken-clad valley. The path steepens for a while before you reach a slight break in the slope. As the path emerges onto a broad spur of the hillside, the bracken is replaced by heather and you continue climbing on a broad, stony track. In mist, you should note that the track actually misses the summit of Black Combe, so remember to bear right across the final grassy dome of the hill. There is a trig point at 1,970ft and a

drystone shelter-cairn in case you need to take shelter from coastal gales.

3 Enjoy the all-round views of the Lakeland fells, Pennines, maybe even Wales, the Isle of Man, Scotland and Ireland. However, the top may be obscured by a woolly cap of cloud. Descend north-eastwards to reach a sudden rocky edge riven with gullies. Walk alongside this edge to descend gradually towards a broad gap lying between Black Combe and White Combe, which is usually a bit boggy.

4 Turn right on the gap and pick up a grooved pathway across the slopes of White Combe. This route describes a sweeping zigzag as it descends into the valley, then makes another zigzag before crossing a beck. Continue downstream along a delightful green track to reach Whicham Mill. Join the access road at the mill and follow it down past Ralliss to reach the main A595 road.

5 Turn right to follow the A595 road back to Whicham church. There is, unfortunately, no way to avoid this closing road walk, but the pastoral Whicham Valley is pleasant enough and you'll soon be back at Whicham church. Walkers who arrived by train have a little further to go to reach Silecroft.

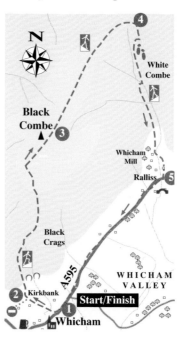

Left: Black Combe seen from Askam, with the familiar cloud cap

ALONG THE WAY

Black Combe's poor quality slate bedrock is the base layer for the Lake District. It outcrops again around Skiddaw and also across the sea on the Isle of Man. The position of Black Combe on a peninsula in the Irish Sea makes it an ideal viewpoint for studying the low-lying Cumbria coast. There is now a continuous coastal path which is best seen from this lofty perch. The railway through South Cumbria is possibly one of the most scenic lines in Britain.

FACT FILE

Distance 7½ miles
Time 4–5 hours
Maps OS Landranger 96, OS Pathfinder 625
Start Whicham Church, grid ref 136827
Terrain Mostly clear paths, except across the summit of the hill
Nearest town Millom
Parking Whicham church
Refreshments Whicham
Public transport British Rail serves nearby Silecroft station
Stiles None
Suitable for Older children and dogs, but take care on exposed summit in mist or foul weather

SCALE FORCE IN STYLE

This complete circuit of Crummock Water includes a visit to a waterfall and a short fellwalk too.

1 Starting from the car park in Buttermere village, follow the track which is signposted for Scale Force. This leads across the flat fields between Buttermere and Crummock Water. Turn right to reach Scale Bridge, then right again after crossing it. Follow a stony path through woodland then climb gradually up a wet and rocky fellside where cairns show the way towards Scale Force.

2 It is difficult to see Scale Force properly as it is hidden in a deep and dark gorge. Follow Scale Beck downstream and forge across a boggy area to reach the shore of Crummock Water. Aim for Ling Crags - a hump of rock that is fixed to the shore by a sweeping bank of gravel.

3 Follow a rather patchy shoreline path across the lower slopes of Mellbreak. This continues through fields and along a concrete wall by the lake. There is a bridge across the inflowing Park Beck and across

the outflowing River Cocker. keep turning right after crossing the Cocker and follow a track through Lanthwaite Woods. This later runs as a field path to reach the B5289 road on Cinderdale Common.

4 Turn right to walk along the road. It is unfenced so that you can walk on the common. Be sure to drift up to the left after crossing Cinderdale Beck, then walk into the secret valley of Rannerdale and follow Squat Beck upstream. Climb from this dale onto a crest which overlooks the fells fringing Buttermere.

5 You can turn right on this crest and walk down the fellside to return to Buttermere village. However, you can also turn sharply right and follow the hummocky crest to the 1,160 ft summit of Rannerdale Knotts. This will take you an extra half-hour. There are two pubs in Buttermere village where you can refresh yourself at the end of the day's walk.

FACT FILE

Distance 9 miles **Time** 5 hours
Maps OS Landranger 89, OS Outdoor Leisure 4, Harvey's Walkers Map and Superwalker of North West Lakeland
Start/parking Buttermere village, grid ref 175170
Terrain Fairly easy, lake and fell paths, but sometimes wet
Nearest towns Cockermouth and Keswick
Refreshments Buttermere village or off-route at Loweswater village
Public transport CMS Buses, tel 01946 63222
Stiles Only a few and not difficult for dogs
Suitable for Older children and dogs on leads

ALONG THE WAY

Victorian travellers used to approach Scale Force in grand style. First they sailed across the head of Crummock Water on boats, then walked up the fellside with their picnic hampers to reach Scale Force. There was a ladder by-passing the lower falls so that people could climb into the deep dark narrow gorge and see the waterfall properly. At 170ft, this is the longest single-leap fall in the Lake District. Unfortunately, the ladder has long since been removed. Today's visitors sometimes scramble up the lower fall, but discover that the water entering their sleeves finds a ready exit from the bottom of their trousers!

Haystacks can be seen from nearby Buttermere village

MAGNIFICENT MOORLAND

Take a walk over heathery moorland to Pundershaw, in Wark Forest, and back by minor roads and field paths on the Pennine Way. This walk has both long and short options.

1 At Dunterley turn up the single track road to Wark, then turn right onto the first farm road. Pass three farms on the right and just before a gate at High Woodhead turn left on a rough track.

2 When the track swings left keep ahead, with a wall on the right, to a wicket gate in the corner. Go through and head up the rough field to a gate in the top right hand corner. Beyond the gate bear slightly right on a faint wheeled track through the heather for about ⅓ mile.

3 Just before you come to a cross wall turn right on another green track, with the wall now on your left. Go through the first field gate on the left, where there is a bridlepath sign.

4 The track goes ahead, just to the right of a shallow dip, over two more hills and hollows. Aim for the farmhouse on the edge of the forest. You come to a long slope down to a gate onto a single track road.

5 Almost opposite is a sign for Pundershaw, the track plunging into newly planted forest. Follow it up and down over two fords to a forestry road. Turn left here and follow it for 1 mile to a junction, where you turn left onto a better road.

6 At the next junction turn right and for a shorter walk turn left at the next junction onto a single track road back to Dunterley. For the longer walk go ahead at the junction into a dip. Just before the bridge turn left to Bridge House Farm.

7 Keep to the right of the farm, through a gate alongside a burn, climbing high above it. At the top go through a gate on the left. Walk through a field, with a hedge on your right, to Esp Mill. Keep left to join a metalled road to Shitlington Hall.

8 You are now on the Pennine Way. Follow the signs left, behind the farm, then right up the fields. Keeping to the right of a high-perched cottage, cross a rough road and make for Shitlington Crags and a slanting path up left.

9 The path goes over the moor ahead to come out at a stile just to the left of a mast. Turn left here, leaving the Pennine Way, and head along a rough road. Turn right at the next junction to walk back down to Dunterley.

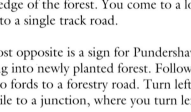

FACT FILE

Distance 7 miles or 5½ miles
Time 3½ hours or 2 hours
Maps OS Landrangers 80 and 87
Start Dunterley Farmhouse on the Bellingham/Hesleyside road, grid ref 826832
Terrain Hilly, some rough walking
Nearest town Bellingham
Parking On verge of Wark road at Dunterley
Refreshments The Hadrian at Wark. Bellingham has pubs and a café at the information centre
Public transport Tyne Valley bus service from Hexham to Bellingham runs past the Dunterley Road, tel 01434 602217

Stiles 2 wooden ones
Suitable for Children. Dogs should be kept on a lead near stock

ALONG THE WAY

The base and shaft of an old cross were restored a few years ago in a field to the left of the road at point 5 of the walk, grid ref 819798.

In 1528 Willie o' Shotlyngton led a raid into Durham, but he received his come-uppance when the whole county rose against him and he was hanged at Hexham. Walkers will be relieved to know that this area is more peaceful today.

Looking across open moorland to the town of Bellingham, near this walk

LAND OF SINGING WATERS

Walk through the delightful upper Breamish Valley, one of several formed by burns that rush down from the Cheviot range. Make your way across moorland grass and heather and stony hillsides where views constantly change.

1 From Hartside Farm turn right onto a gated road to Alnhammoor. Just past the farm go through a field gate on the left. Head right down the field to a stile halfway down the fence, then on to a plank bridge over a burn. Slant right up the grassy hillside.

2 Down to the left is the Shank Burn. Start moving gradually away from it, aiming for a gate on the horizon. Adequate waymarks take you on to the right of Little Dodd's summit to a cross-paths, 1¾ miles from Alnhammoor.

3 Turn right onto a bridleway between Shillmoor and Cushat Law. Half a mile further on it becomes a definite track down to Low Bleakhope. Cross the burn and turn right before the farm bungalow onto the valley road. For the shorter walk turn right again and head back to the start (3 miles).

4 For a longer, more strenuous walk, turn left to High Bleakhope. Walk ahead through two pine plantations to a cabin and sheepfold (¾ mile). From here slant back to the right to a wicket in the top corner. Head up the next hill, slightly right, to a fence, and then turn right.

5 Continue to a junction with another fence on the left. Pass this and step over the fence. Ahead, over to the right, are two low mounds. Make for the grassy one on the left over some soggy moorland. At the top there is a cairn on the right, while Great Standrop, Hedgehope and Cheviot are on the left.

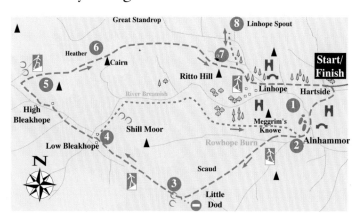

6 Walk ahead into the heather, aiming for a steep fall of cliffs at the foot of a huge hill (Dunmoor). Continue until you see a fence and two gates, then make for the right-hand gate.

7 Go through the gate and round the flank of Ritto Hill. Slant slowly down to the left to a wicket in a fence on the left, then onto a rough red track. Turn right and follow it back to Hartside.

8 For Linhope Spout turn left and follow the track by the wood, then over a field, where it is well-signed, to the waterfall (½ mile). Return the same way.

ALONG THE WAY

The bridleway used in Section 3 is part of the Salters' Way, an ancient track that eventually crosses into Scotland. Until the 14th century it was called the Thieves' Road. There are many ancient settlements on the flanks of the hills, including Ritto Hill and Greeves Ash. Linhope Spout, at 56ft high, is one of Northumberland's loveliest waterfalls.

FACT FILE

Distance 7 miles (6 miles with an extra mile to Linhope Spout or 3 mile option)
Time 4 hours or 3 hours
Maps OS Landranger 81
Start/parking Hartside Farm up the Breamish Valley, grid ref 975162
Terrain Hilly. Some rough moorland walking on the long walk with no defined path, but plenty of landmarks
Nearest town Wooler
Refreshments None on route
Public transport None
Stiles 1 wooden one
Suitable for Children. Dogs on leads near stock

Make a detour near the end of the walk to visit Lanhope Spout

A view into Oxendale from the walk along Blea Rigg

Fact File

Distance 10 miles

Time 5 hours

Maps OS Landranger 90; OS Outdoor Leisure 6 & 7; Harveys Walkers Map and

Superwalker Map of Western Lakeland

Start/parking Elterwater village, grid ref 328048

Terrain Moderate fellwalking and easier valley paths

Nearest town Ambleside

Refreshments Elterwater and Dungeon Ghyll

Public transport CMS Buses, tel 01946 63222

Stiles A couple towards the end

Suitable for Older children and dogs on leads

THE LONG VALLEY

Enjoy a walk around Langdale and a dramatic spot for lunch.

1 Leave Elterwater village as if going to Ambleside but when you reach the B5343 road cross it and walk uphill across the bracken-strewn common. Cross a minor road and follow another path further uphill to a gap between two low fells. Turn left to climb up along the hummocky spur leading towards Dow Bank.

2 Although there is a fairly clear path along the broad crest passing Dow Bank, Silver How, Lang How and Castle How, there are also other paths and, in misty weather, this rather hummocky terrain can be confusing. In clear weather, however, you should have no problem navigating in stages as you climb towards Blea Rigg, enjoying the rugged little tops and tiny pools of water hidden among the fells. Pause to enjoy the view on Blea Rigg at 1,776ft.

3 Beyond Blea Rigg, you should head off to the left and follow a path down to Stickle Tarn, which is beneath the huge rockface of Pavey Ark. It's a dramatic place to stop for lunch but in bad weather you should walk down alongside Mill Gill on a solid, reconstructed path and take a break in the shelter of the Sticklebarn Tavern. You could also cut the walk short at this point and catch a bus back to either Elterwater or Ambleside.

4 To continue the walk, cross the B5343 road and follow a short farm access road to Side House, then turn left to follow a fellside path across the lower slopes of Lingmoor Fell. This rough path leads to another farmhouse called Oak Howe, where you can follow a clearer track around the steep fellside to reach Baysbrown Farm.

5 Follow a narrow road uphill from Baysbrown Farm into a wood. Keep to the road and a descent is followed by two left turns back into Elterwater village. The Britannia Inn awaits to quench the thirst you have worked up during this circuit.

ALONG THE WAY

Langdale is a pure Norse name and simply means Long Valley. This is how it appears in the view from Blea Rigg, as it snakes from the high fells towards Windermere. In fact, many place names in the area are Norse, including: fell (hill); gill (ravine); rigg (ridge); mere (lake); thwaite (clearing); and beck (stream). The county name of Cumbria, however, belongs to an earlier language closely allied to Welsh. The Cumbria Way passes through Langdale on route from Ulverston to Carlisle.

WOODS AND THE WEAR

Starting at the old bridge over the Wear at Croxdale, take a high route over fields to Shincliffe, and then return through bluebell woods.

1 Follow the drive through the park, over a cattle grid and bridge. About 200yds on, turn right up some steps, going on to rejoin the road. Turn right. Follow the road round to the left, past the old church on the left to a junction by some huge barns. Turn right for High Croxdale.

2 If you want to avoid ploughed fields, carry on to the farm. Go round to the front and turn right over a field to a spinney and on to a bridleway. Turn left and rejoin the walk at point 6.

3 Cross the stile on the right at the end of the trees (¼ mile), down the field into a wood to steps going up left to a stile (¼ mile). Head out across the field parallel to the wooded cutting down on the right.

4 Swing up left, just before a fence, to a dilapidated barn. Go round behind it, crossing two stiles, back into the next field. Go down the field to the trees and turn left for ¼ mile. When you see, ahead of you to the left, the point where a fence and hedge meet, aim for the gap at the corner.

5 The path should go through the gap and down beside the hedge on the right, but the way out is blocked by a fence, so go down the other side of the hedge to a gate onto a lane.

6 Turn left onto the gated bridleway (where point 2 joins up) and follow it for 1 mile. At a junction cross the metalled road into a footpath. It joins a rough road at a junction. Turn left for West Grange.

7 Follow the signs past the farm and turn left immediately down a field to woods. Turn right along the edge to a stile into them, to come out on the lane to Shincliffe Hall.

8 The track narrows after the Hall and slants up to the left, switchbacking through wooded banks to High Buttersby. Turn right here for Croxdale Wood House, on a good road.

9 Just before the House a path on the right slants left into the woods to Low Buttersby. Turn left when it emerges from the trees onto a gated road which rejoins the previous one. Turn right here and walk back through the park to the start.

ALONG THE WAY

The old Norman church at Croxdale Hall is no longer in use. Just past it are some magnificent Victorian farm buildings. Shincliffe Hall is now part of Durham University. About 2 miles away from Croxdale, on the road into Durham City, are the Botanic Gardens, which are worth a visit.

Pass this disused Norman church at Croxdale Hall

FACT FILE

Distance 8 miles
Time 4 hours
Maps OS Landrangers 88 and 93
Start/parking Either side of the old bridge over the Wear at Croxdale. Start at park gates just beyond the bridge. Grid ref 266376
Terrain Easy, although the ploughed fields and paths through the woods can be muddy and slippery
Nearest town Durham
Refreshments The Bridge, Croxdale; the Cock of the North (1 mile nearer Durham)
Public transport Buses from Durham and Darlington. Passengers alight at The Bridge in Croxdale. Take the Brandon Road, turn first left down the dead-end road to the old bridge and park gates
Stiles Several wooden ones and one hurdle
Suitable for Children, dogs on leads

A FERTILE PLAIN

Walk alongside the River Tees and then strike out over open countryside in this lovely part of Teesdale.

1 Go through the metal gate and follow the riverside path to High Coniscliffe for 3 miles, sometimes between the trees, sometimes along the edge of a field, crossing three stiles on the way. The path swings up right just after you see the steeple among some trees on the right.

2 When you reach the road, cross it and turn right. At the end of the village turn left by the Spotted Dog pub onto a bridleway, past the Mill House and over two fields. Turn left at a wall ahead and cross five fields to the B6279.

3 Cross into a farm road to Low Walworth. At the bridge just before the farm, ignore the 'diverted sign'. Follow the bridleway signs through farm buildings, but go ahead at the diesel tank. Turn down the righthand side of the field to a gateway on the right.

4 Cross the ploughed field to a stile. Cross it and a footbridge, then keep down to the right side of the next field to cross a hurdle and the next meadow to a plank bridge in the bottom right corner.

5 Cross and go forward, heading slightly left to Archdeacon Newton Farm. Follow the footpath signs through it onto the farm road and take the second bridleway sign, walking parallel to the A1 for 500yds. Turn left under it and then immediately right for another 500yds to the B6279.

6 Turn left for 100yds then right up a road to Coniscliffe Grange. Keep to the left of the farm and follow the bridleway for 1 mile to the A67. Turn right and cross at the left sign for Low Coniscliffe to walk back to the start (¼mile) through the village.

Enjoy the open expanses of Teesdale countryside

FACT FILE

Distance 9 miles
Time 4½ hours
Map OS Landranger 93
Start/parking Low Coniscliffe, grid ref 248136. Turn left at west end of village. Limited parking at bottom of lane near river
Terrain Easy, flat, ploughed fields – may be muddy
Nearest town Darlington
Refreshments Duke of Wellington, High Coniscliffe (turn left instead of right at point 2)
Public transport Buses from Darlington
Stiles Four, one hurdle to climb
Suitable for Children. Dogs on leads in places

ALONG THE WAY

The Tees at Low Coniscliffe is a placid, middle-aged river - gone is its upland verve and dash. The flat, fertile plain spreads out on either side.

High Coniscliffe church is the only one in England dedicated to the Saxon King Edwin. Thornton Hall, the tall, gabled house that can be seen from the fields at point 3, dates from Elizabethan times.

POET'S FAVOURITE

The Duddon Valley is surrounded by rugged little fells, clothed in patchy woodlands and watered by a powerful rocky river.

1 Start in the tiny hamlet of Seathwaite at the Newfield Inn. There is a gate on a corner of the road just to one side of the inn, where a stony track leads into Newfield Wood. When the track emerges above the wood, it continues up a rugged fellside on the slopes of Caw, and you can enjoy the views which unfold across the dale.

2 The track passes through a gap on the shoulder of Caw, then starts to descend towards the farmstead of Hoses. Don't go down to the farm, but head up to the right and aim for the top of a minor road. When you reach the road, you can also climb to the rugged 1,231ft summit of Stickle Pike as an extra. The views across Southern Lakeland make the short climb worth the effort.

3 Walk down the road back into the Duddon Valley. At first the road is unfenced, but below Kiln Bank it is flanked by a monumental drystone wall. Huge boulders have been stacked one on top of another to rise well above your head.

4 Cross the road bridge on the left at Hall Dunnerdale, then immediately turn right to follow the access road to Wallowbarrow Farm. Study the various agricultural implements before you go straight through the farmyard and continue along a path into a wooded area. You will reach a packhorse bridge spanning the River Duddon and you have a choice of routes at this point.

5 Crossing the bridge allows you to return to Seathwaite early. However, if you don't cross the bridge you can trace the powerful River Duddon upstream through Wallowbarrow Gorge. A path has been built across a bouldery slope and it eventually climbs high above the river before descending to the Fickle Steps.

6 The Fickle Steps are huge stepping stones across the River Duddon. When you cross them you can climb up to a minor road and turn right. The road leads back to Seathwaite, though you should pause to admire several waterfalls where the road runs alongside Tarn Beck.

ALONG THE WAY

The poet Norman Nicholson described the Duddon Valley as 'my favourite place of all. There is such variety, such texture. Every three weeks in the year it's a different place.' The leisurely approach is to ride with the postman and use the Post Bus service from Broughton, but study the timetable carefully in advance. The Newfield Inn is the place to relax for food and drink after the walk is over.

Pause to look at the waterfalls on Tarn Beck, on the way back to Seathwaite

FACT FILE

Distance 8 miles (or 6)
Time 4 – 5 hours
Maps OS Landranger 96, OS Outdoor Leisure 6, Harveys Walker's and Superwalker Maps of Southern Lakeland
Start Newfield Inn, Seathwaite, grid ref 227960
Terrain Simple fell and valley walking on good paths
Nearest town Millom
Parking Limited – try near the chapel
Refreshments Newfield Inn, Seathwaite
Public transport Post Bus, tel 01229 716220
Stiles None
Suitable for Older children and dogs on leads

YORKSHIRE AND HUMBERSIDE

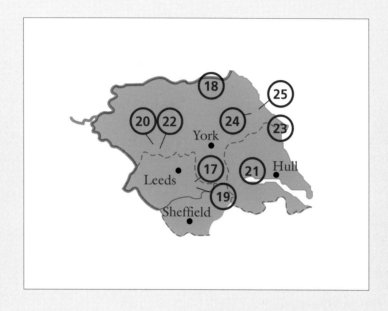

CALL OF THE WILD

Brockadale boasts a nature reserve teeming with plant life. Enjoy a late summer stroll through this glorious countryside.

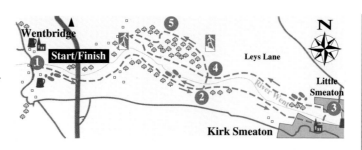

1 After parking the car walk south along the main street, crossing the River Went, and find the path between the cottages on the left hand side of the road, opposite a road junction. The path crosses meadows and takes you under the massive arches supporting the Great North Road to enter a wood over a stile. Follow the path through the wood, sometimes walking alongside the river as it meanders down the valley.

2 Head into a meadow and continue straight ahead, ignoring the paths to the right and left. You can shorten the walk here by turning left and crossing the bridge, then heading left over the stile at point 4. The meadow is managed by the Yorkshire Wildlife Trust and the bank on the right is a mass of cowslips and orchids in spring. Cross the next stile into another wood. You soon reach more meadows – continue straight over these, crossing more stiles until the path rises to the road in the village of Kirk Smeaton.

3 At the road turn left and walk towards the church. When the road turns right carry straight on through an iron kissing gate and follow the path round the left hand side of the church. Notice that all four windows on that side are differently shaped. Cross the stone stile into the lane and turn left to cross the river, rising to reach Chapel Lane at Little Smeaton. Turn left for 50yds to reach a stile and gate alongside the old chapel. Follow the path along the top of Smeaton Craggs and re-enter the land managed by the Yorkshire Wildlife Trust. Cross the field beyond and approach Hunter's Bridge which spans the river.

4 Don't cross the bridge, but climb the stile to the right and walk upstream for about 75yds to a cattle drink. Turn half-right uphill and make for a stile by the notice board on the edge of the wood. Enter the wood and carry straight on uphill to meet another path at a T-junction. Turn right and follow this path round the wood, ignoring paths to right and left, and drop down to meet a lane (Leys Lane). Turn left and continue on the lane until a gap appears in the wire fence on the left.

5 Go through the gap and follow the path uphill. This area is known as the Butterfly Ride. At the top, by a seat, turn right and walk to the edge of the wood. Carry on ahead and in 150yds, on a right bend, turn left down a track through the wood past a cottage and a wooden shed, into a meadow. Continue ahead alongside the wood and cross the stile to reach Hunter's Bridge. Cross this, turning left across the field and right at the junction to re-enter the wood and retrace your steps to Wentbridge.

FACT FILE

Distance 9 miles
Time 4 hours
Maps OS Landranger 111, OS Pathfinder 704
Start/parking Wentbridge village, grid ref 488174. Cars can be left by the roadside
Terrain Easy, only slight gradients
Nearest town Pontefract
Refreshments Blue Bell in Wentbridge, café in Wentbridge, opposite the start of the walk, pubs and cafés in Pontefract
Public transport Yorkshire Rider, tel 01132 457676; there is also a bus service between Doncaster and Wentbridge, tel 01302 344414 and between Pontefract and Wentbridge, tel 01977 703366
Stiles Several, not difficult
Suitable for Children. Dogs on leads in nature reserve

ALONG THE WAY

Brockadale is referred to as Broken Dale on the early OS maps. A railway once ran through the valley with a branch line to the quarries in Brockadale. Some of the dale is now managed by the Yorkshire Wildlife Trust. The undergrowth at Butterfly Ride was cut back to create a wide, sunlit area. Bushes were planted to attract butterflies and specimens to be seen include Red Admiral, Peacock, Comma and Wall Brown.

COLD COMFORT

This tough walk over Urra Moor and Cold Moor is rewarded with outstanding views into County Durham and across the Cleveland Hills to Roseberry Topping and the sea.

1 There is a good car park at the top of Clay Bank but on a fine day it soon becomes full. There is alternative parking available on the wide grass verge. From here, walk along the road towards Bilsdale, heading south. In a couple of hundred yards turn left through a gate, following a sign for the Cleveland Way. It is quite a climb along this well-defined footpath with a short scramble onto the moor, although there is an alternative route on the left. Once you are out on the moor keep to the wide path straight ahead.

2 This path is used for three long distance walks, the Cleveland Way, the Lyke Wake Walk and Wainwright's Coast to Coast. The view over the Cleveland Hills presents the unusual shape of Roseberry Topping and the monument to the local seafarer Captain Cook. In 2 miles turn right along a wide track just before the white triangulation station. Then in about 1 mile, where the wide track goes left, take the bridleway straight ahead through the heather and then down the hill. Go straight down the steep track and through a gate or stile in the stone wall.

3 The path meanders along to the road via two farm gates. Turn left here down the hill over the bridge across Bilsdale Beck and into Seave Green at the main road. Turn left along the roadside footpath for a few hundred yards to Chop Gate (pronouced Chop Yat). If you want to visit the Buck Inn keep straight on into the village. Otherwise, turn right opposite the war memorial onto the Carlton road, then immediately right again past the chapel along the public bridleway. This long uphill path can be quite overgrown in summer and eventually exits onto Cold Moor through a gate.

4 Follow the worn track north over the top of Cold Moor, eventually reaching the escarpment edge at Broughton Bank. Turn right at the junction to follow the Cleveland Way again down a steep, eroded hill under repair.

Pass through the gate at the bottom and go straight ahead towards the impressive Wainstones at the top of the opposite hill – they will be silhouetted against the sky.

5 The Wainstones, pronounced locally as Wainsteeans, is a magnificent outcrop of rocks that seems to be balanced precariously on the edge of the moor. There are challenging rock faces for climbers, with the Sphinx Rock standing proud on the Bilsdale face. Legend says that a Danish chieftain was murdered here. There is a choice of routes now – you can either take the short but exhilarating scramble through the heart of the stones or follow the path round to the left.

6 At the summit stop to admire the view north to Teesside, Durham and Newcastle, or west across to the Yorkshire Dales. Cross Hasty Bank top then in 1 mile turn sharp left through the rocks and down a steep hill to a stile on the left. Cross the stile and follow the Cleveland Way sign down a narrow path to the road. Turn left to return to the Clay Bank car park.

FACT FILE

Distance 9½ miles
Time 4–5 hours
Maps OS Landranger 93 and 94, OS Outdoor Leisure 26
Start Clay Bank, grid ref 572036
Terrain Mainly good moorland tracks but sometimes stony and eroded. Can be muddy, if wet, climbing up from Chop Gate. There are two strenuous uphill sections
Nearest town Guisborough
Parking Car park at Clay Bank for 50 cars, otherwise park on wide verge
Refreshments The Buck Inn at Chop Gate (further into the village, slightly off route)
Public transport Bus service operates Fridays only, tel 01642 710324
Stiles Two, easy
Suitable for Agile adults and strong children. Dogs under firm control on the grouse moor

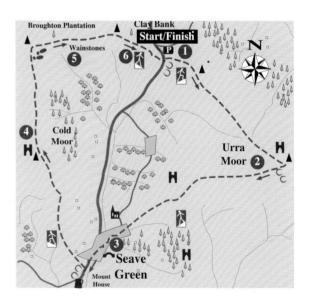

ALONG THE WAY

The Wainstones, an impressive outcrop of rock, stands silhouetted against the sky on the approach from Cold Moor. The moors contrast with the lush Bilsdale Valley which was little known when farming was first introduced here by Cistercian monks. Iron ore was smelted and mined, and as late as 1900 a Smith still produced his own iron in the valley. Jet and coal mining boomed for a long time and you may see the scars as you cross the moors.

ANCIENT CIVILISATIONS

Take a walk along paths and trackways around ancient settlements in pleasant countryside.

1 Begin by walking along Darning Lane from the B6474 (Thorpe Lane), passing West Farm and turning right along Garth Lane. Where the lane turns left keep straight on along a track. At the end of this pass through the right-hand gateway and walk along the edge of the field with the hedge on your right. Walk towards the barn ahead and when you reach the field edge turn left, with a hedge on your right, to a bridge at the top of the field. Pothills Marsh is on the left.

2 Cross the bridge and go straight ahead, keeping the hedge on your left, until you reach another footbridge. Cross this and turn right, then in about 20yds turn left, with a hedge on your left. Continue uphill to the top of the field. Turn right and after 20yds go left over a stile. Continue walking uphill with the wood now on your right. At the top look back to admire the view. Keep going straight ahead, over the stile and into a grassy lane. At the end turn right, with the sports field on the right and houses on the left, to reach the road.

3 At the road turn right, past Beacon Hill on the right, and turn right again along a bridleway beside two old cottages – keep these on your left. Upton Beacon was the site of an Armada Beacon in the 1580s, to warn of the approach of the Spanish Armada and was later used in the Napoleonic Wars. Now a water tower has replaced it.

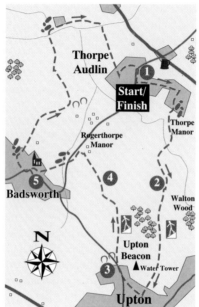

4 Keep along the bridleway; walk downhill and carry on at a junction, with a hedge on your left, to reach a stile and gate. Continue past Rogerthorpe Manor to the road. Turn left here, crossing the road after 50yds to take a path on the right to Badsworth. Follow the path through two more kissing gates into the churchyard. Walk around the church to reach the road. The church of St Mary is mentioned in the Domesday Book but only a few of the Norman features remain.

5 Turn right and follow the road round a left-hand bend, passing Badsworth Hall. The original building was demolished in 1941 and only the stabling hall remains. Turn right into Ninevah Lane and take the second right into Grove Lane until you reach some farm buildings. Take the right-hand fork at the end of the buildings (Firthfield Lane). When you reach the T-junction turn left and follow the track to the River Went. A modern farm bridge lies alongside the old packhorse bridge. Immediately after crossing the bridge turn right and walk downstream, with the river on your right, until you reach another footbridge. Cross this and, keeping the hedge on your left, walk towards the houses. Turn left at the road to reach the B6474 and turn right to arrive back at the start in Darning Lane.

ALONG THE WAY

Pothills Marsh is a Site of Special Scientific Interest and a good place to look for a short-eared owl or toads, frogs and dragonflies in the summer. Rogerthorpe Manor, built around 1600, is said to be haunted by a phantom cavalier and a naughty Victorian child who rattles windows and opens cupboards. Badsworth, or Baddesworth, was first recorded in the Domesday Book.

FACT FILE

Distance 7½ miles
Time 3 hours
Maps OS Landranger 110, OS Pathfinder 704
Start/parking Darning Lane, Thorpe Audlin, a T-junction with B6474, grid ref 475160
Terrain Easy, only slight gradients. Muddy in places after rain
Nearest town Pontefract
Refreshments Fox & Hounds, Thorpe Audlin
Public transport Buses run from Pontefract to Doncaster and Pontefract to Barnsley via Upton. Tel 0113 2457676 for information
Stiles Several, nothing difficult
Suitable for Children and dogs

Rogerthorpe Manor dates from the early 17th century and is thought to be haunted by ghosts

Cone-shaped Sharp Haw is the summit of a long ridge

FOREST AND FELL

This route combines pleasant forest tracks with the ascent of Flasby Fell, which offers wide views of the moors between Wharfedale and Malhamdale

1 From the start, walk south-east down the road, around three sharp bends. Eventually you reach Tarn House Farm on the left. About 50yds beyond the farm climb a stile by a gate on the right, signposted Flasby 2½. Cross the field, with a fence on your left to climb another stile by a gate. Continue with the fence on the left until you reach a wooden stile in this fence; cross the stile and continue in the same direction as before, with the fence now on your right. Pass two gates with stone stiles. From the second of these gates, walk along the top of a raised bank full of rabbit holes. Then bear right to cross a stream by a ford. Cross the field to a gate into the forest; there is a prominent white-painted grounded trailer by this gate.

2 Follow the path into the forest for about 100yds until it meets the main forest track. Turn left. Follow this forest road for about 1 mile, bearing right when the track forks after about ¼ mile.

3 Where the track goes round a sharp hairpin bend to the left, follow a footpath signposted Flasby 1¼. This goes straight on through some rhododendrons and soon joins a track coming down from the right. Turn left onto this track signposted Flasby 1, and follow it to the end of the forest. The track now curves left as it goes downhill, through a field

to a gate. Go through the gate, across the bridge and follow the track down to Flasby Hall Farm.

4 Turn right and walk up the lane – don't bear left on the footpath to Rylstone. At the end of the track go through a gate into a field and carry straight on up the field with the wall on the right, to a second gate. Carry on up the path, keeping the wall on the right, to a saddle (ridge between two summits). On the saddle, immediately opposite a gate in the wall, turn left and climb a steep path through the bracken to the summit of Rough Haw.

5 From Rough Haw, retrace your steps to the gate in the wall, and climb the ladder stile to the left of the gate. The ground can be very muddy here. Follow the footpath climbing up the side of the fell to the trig point on the summit of Sharp Haw.

6 Turn left and climb a ladder stile to the south-east of Sharp Haw's summit, and follow the path down a broad, grassy ridge. There are a few marker posts where the path is indistinct. When the path joins a rough lane, turn left and follow the lane back to the starting point.

ALONG THE WAY

Flasby Fell has two summits, Sharp Haw and Rough Haw; they are very different in character, despite being separated by only a short distance. Sharp Haw appears as a cone from most directions, and is the summit of a long ridge, while Rough Haw is more rounded. There is a hollowed-out wind shelter on the summit of Rough Haw – an ideal place for lunch. The views from both summits are extensive.

FACT FILE

Distance 7 miles
Time 3½ hours
Maps OS Landranger 103, OS Outdoor Leisure 10
Start On a bend on the minor road north-east of Stirton, near Tarn House, grid ref 976539
Terrain Distinct paths and tracks for virtually the whole route: two short, steep gradients, but most climbing is quite gentle; one very muddy path
Nearest town Skipton
Parking Space for a few cars at the start; space for four cars on the B6265 opposite the minor road just north of the Craven

Heifer, grid ref 982537 – a footpath goes west from this point to join the walk at the third bend on the road just after the start. There is also space for five or six cars just south of the road junction at grid ref 978541 – walk up the minor road to Stirton to join the route
Refreshments None
Public transport Bus route 71, Skipton railway station to Grassington, passes the Craven Heifer hourly from about 10am Mon-Sat in summer, but only two suitable buses on Sundays and Bank Holidays. Limited service in

winter. Operated by Pride of the Dales, tel 01756 7531323
Stiles Several, varied, including ladder stiles over walls
Suitable for Children and dogs that can cope with stiles

There are 87 steps to climb in Elloughton Dale, although they can be avoided

ALONG THE WAY

Wauldby Manor and Church are all that remain of Wauldby village, one of the many Wolds villages to disappear following depopulation since the 15th century with the change to sheep farming. Look out for deer among the trees above Brantingham and Elloughton Dales.

FACT FILE

Distance 11 or 14 miles
Time 5 or 7 hours
Map OS Landranger 106
Start Brantingham village, grid ref 940294
Terrain Can be muddy in places
Nearest town Beverley
Parking By the village green, Brantingham

Refreshments Triton Inn, Brantingham. Also Skidby Mill Restaurant and the Half Moon Inn, Skidby village
Public transport East Yorks 155 Hull-South Cave and 143 Brough-Beverley serve Brantingham
Stiles Few
Suitable for Everyone

THE FORGOTTEN VILLAGE

Walk through a string of attractive villages between the Yorkshire Wolds and the shoreline of the Humber and visit a village that has practically disappeared.

1 Before you set off, spend a few minutes looking at the information board on the green by the phone box. From here, walk into the village and by the old water pump take the narrow lane to the right. This climbs quite steeply up Spout Hill onto the Wolds. At the top of the hill a stile on the right leads into woodland. Follow this path through the belt of woodland above Brantingham for about ½ mile to where it descends alongside a fence to meet a track. Turn right along this track but almost immediately look out for an indistinct path that continues steeply down through the trees on the left. Climb over a stile onto the roadside.

2 Turn left up the minor road through Elloughton Dale. In a few yards a clear path on the right climbs up through the trees to a waymarked post at a junction of paths. Alternatively, about 200yds up the road, a sign points the way, to the right, up 87 steep steps through the trees to the same point. From the waymarked post continue on a clear path, not shown on the current OS map, through another narrow strip of trees to a gate on to the Welton road. Turn left up the road past some riding stables. At the edge of the wood on the right you come to the concrete access road to Welton Wold Farm. Turn right here along the signed footpath by the side of this road. At the trees near the top of a slight rise, turn left on the Wolds Way towards Wauldby Manor.

3 By the pond at Wauldby Manor continue straight on past some farmhouses. The path curves round the edge of fields to meet a junction of tracks. Go straight on, leaving the Wolds Way, and follow the farm track through York Grounds Farm to a road. Cross over, turn left and in a few yards turn right at the bridleway sign. Keep to the edge of the field for about ½ mile, eventually joining a farm track near a line of electricity pylons. Across the fields to the left is Rowley Church. About ½ mile down the lane you come to an old railway bridge that once carried the Hull and Barnsley railway line.

For the longer walk to Skidby, carry on under the bridge down the lane into the village. Pass the church and pub and turn right to the windmill. Return via field paths to the cemetery and retrace your steps to the bridge.

4 Near the old railway bridge, a bridleway sign points the way up the side of the field. The right of way keeps by the field boundary to come alongside a wood. The way now becomes an enclosed path between tall hedgerows as it follows a circuitous route around the perimeter of Hessle golf course. It passes some riding stables before turning towards the club house. Head down the driveway to the road. Turn right and follow the road for 1 mile to the junction at Wauldby Green, Raywell. Beware of traffic on this straight, fast stretch of road.

5 Just to the right of the junction cross over and head for Nut Wood on the hill opposite. You can choose to go either side of the wood, or even meander through the wood itself. At the far end you join the track that has passed along the north side of the wood. This follows a shallow valley gradually uphill with more woodland on the right to the junction of paths you encountered earlier (point 3).

6 Continue straight on, following the Wolds Way again. At a road junction cross and head towards Elloughton and then, where the road goes left, walk straight ahead at a Wolds Way sign on a green lane, passing Long Plantation. This brings you to the top of Spout Hill above Brantingham. Go over a stile on your right by the edge of the trees, and descend across pasture towards Brantingham church. Head down the road back into the village, bearing right to return to the green by the village pond.

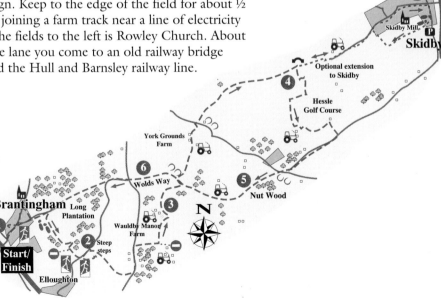

DESOLATE BEAUTY

Enjoy a walk beside the River Wharfe and up the Valley of Desolation,
then climb to heather-covered moorland with fine views.

1 Leave the car park at the north end, turn right and walk 100yds into the village. Turn left along the main road for 50yds, then go right down the driveway to Bolton Priory. Continue to a gate and out onto the road. After 200yds, at the Cavendish Memorial, keep straight on, with the fence on the right, to cross a stile and go down some steps. Walk across the field towards the river, then follow the river upstream to the Cavendish Pavilion café. This is the starting point for the shorter walk.

2 Turn right to cross the wooden bridge over the River Wharfe, then turn immediately left onto the wide path and walk upstream. The path soon bears right and climbs a few stone steps to cross a wooden stile. Take the right fork and climb the path to the road.

3 Turn left up this minor road, climbing a short hill before the road levels off. After about 200yds turn right to a gate by a cottage. Go through this and bear left across the field to another gate, from which a track leads up the valley. This goes over a slight rise and then bends left to descend to the gill. Fork right over the grass to the path up the hillside and round the top of a gully before descending to a bridge across Posforth Gill.

4 Follow the path up the valley with the stream on your right. At a fork bear left and climb to a ladder stile at the edge of a wood. Cross the stile, bear right and follow the wide track through the wood to leave by a gate at the end.

5 The track continues up for nearly 2 miles, over the open moor to the summit of Simon's Seat, becoming a cairned footpath for the last ½ mile. Take care not to turn right half way up the track.

6 From the trig point turn right, along a faint path towards Lord's Seat. This part of the route is quite muddy. When you reach a wall by the outcrop, turn right and follow a footpath alongside it. This becomes a more distinct track as it descends towards Little Agill Beck. Just before the beck the track passes through a gate in the wall and continues along the other side of it for a short distance before swinging back to the right, through another gate, to continue on the right-hand side of the wall.

7 Follow the track through a gate by a stone shelter. The track now climbs a little before levelling off; it then veers to the right away from the wall, crosses a small stream and starts to descend gently across the moor. Ignore a track which joins from the left.

8 For the short route bear right at the next T-junction and follow the track downhill past Bolton Park farm to the road and bridge by the Cavendish Pavilion car park. For the long route bear left at the junction – the track descends to cross a stream at a ford. Continue up the same track, bearing right whenever the track forks, keeping a roughly south-easterly direction and gradually descending towards the Wharfe Valley in front of you.

9 Eventually the track crosses a cattle grid; there is a notice board on the right by a farm entrance giving information about the access area. About 100yds further on, go down a footpath to the right, following a wall on the right, to a minor road at Storiths. Go down the lane opposite the footpath, following it round to the right. Where the road ends at a farm, take a footpath down between two walls until it emerges at the top of a hill above the River Wharfe, with Bolton Priory opposite. Bear right and follow the path downhill to cross the river by the bridge. The path continues across the fields and up some steps to emerge through an archway in a wall at Bolton Abbey.

40

FACT FILE

Distance 11 or 8½ miles
Time 5½ or 4 hours
Maps OS Landranger 104, OS Outdoor Leisure 10
Start/parking Bolton Abbey car park, grid ref 071539
Terrain Distinct paths and tracks, a few short, steep gradients; some muddy stretches. Simon's Seat is best avoided in mist, since navigation at the summit can be tricky and there are steep drops
Nearest town Ilkley
Refreshments Bolton Abbey village; Cavendish Pavilion; Buffers at Storiths

Public transport Early morning school days only bus (Keighley and District route 76) from Skipton returns about 7 hours later. Yorkshire Dales National Park publishes a free booklet giving details of Dales transport
Stiles Three easy ones
Suitable for Older children. Dogs prohibited

ALONG THE WAY

The remains of the Augustinian Bolton Priory are at Bolton Abbey. After the Dissolution, the nave was preserved for lay worship, and is now the local parish church.

The Valley of Desolation got its name in the early19th century, when a severe storm swept away all the trees. There is no evidence of this damage today in this idyllic valley.

NOTE Much of this walk is over permissive paths and land subject to an access agreement between the National Park and the Bolton Abbey Estate. The land is closed on various days in the summer due to fire risk and in the autumn for shooting. Dogs are not allowed on the access land. For information on closure, tel 01756 752774 (Mon–Fri normal office hours) April to October and 01756 752748 November to March.

A glimpse of Wharfedale from Simon's Seat

CLIFFTOPS AND CAVES

Famous for its steep chalk cliffs and a plethora of nesting seabirds, Flamborough Head is full of interest. There are smugglers' caves to explore at low tide.

1 Start from the large car park at North Landing, Flamborough. Walk back along the road through Flamborough village following the signs for Bridlington. Walk through the village, then take the first left after the church. Turn almost immediately right and at the bend in the road cross a stile into a field.

2 Keep on the path which eventually meets a narrow road. Turn left at the road which leads to Danes Dyke car park. Follow the footpath alongside a brick wall, heading downhill into the Dyke. Cross the footbridge and head up the other side, bearing left at the top. In a few yards take the signed path to Sewerby on the right. The path goes across the golf course, so look out for stray balls.

3 At Sewerby walk along the side of the cricket field. You might like to visit Sewerby Hall – the entrance is on the right here. If you want to stop for refreshments, continue ahead into the village. If you only came for the walk go left around the cricket field to the cliff top and turn left again to take the cliff path towards Flamborough.

4 The cliff path rises and falls with the shape of the cliffs and the going can be rough at times, but there is the chance of a paddle to soothe your feet at South Landing. The cliff path is well maintained with steps built into the side of the cliff.

Selwicks Bay is probably the most interesting part of the walk – there are two lighthouses here.

5 The old 'chalk tower' lighthouse was built around 1674 from local chalk. Its light source was a brazier which was lit at the top of the tower. It is possible it was never even used – opinions vary. The modern lighthouse was built in 1806 and was completed by a local builder who constructed the tower, which stands more than 90ft high, without using any scaffolding. Lighthouses, however, are useless in a sea fog, so the building on the cliff top a few hundred yards from the lighthouse contains a foghorn.

6 After visiting the lighthouses return to the cliff path, following signs for North Landing. Look out for the sea birds nesting in the cliffs as you approach North landing. Follow the cliff path back to the car park but allow time to explore the caves on the beach, remembering to watch out for the tide.

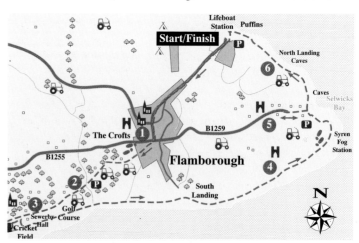

ALONG THE WAY

The caves at North Landing were once used for smuggling. Flamborough had a famous smuggler called Robin Lythe – his cave can be seen at the right-hand side of the cove. Look out for the puffins, razorbills and guillemots on the cliffs. Out at sea you will spot gannets flying to their nesting places at Bempton, a little further along.

FACT FILE

Distance 9 miles
Time 3½ hours
Map OS Landranger 101
Start North Landing, Flamborough, grid ref 239720
Terrain Well-maintained cliff paths with steep steps up and down to the bays
Nearest town Bridlington
Parking Large free car park at North Landing, Flamborough
Refreshments Pub and café at Sewerby and café and restaurant at North Landing
Public transport There is an hourly service from Bridlington from the East Yorkshire bus station in Princess Street
Stiles One, easy
Suitable for All, with care and close supervision of children. The cliffs are high and sheer and the paths to the bays, although, well maintained, are steep

MOORLAND MEMORIAL

On the edge of Levisham Moor overlooking beautiful Newtondale is the folly known as Skelton Tower. Skelton was lord of the manor in 1840 and owned most of the land around here. Could the tower be his memorial?

1 Park carefully in Levisham village, signed off the Pickering to Whitby road, (or take the steam train from Pickering to Levisham station). Leave the village on the road you arrived on and shortly after the double bend follow the 'Link' sign along a bridleway on the right. At the bottom of the hill keep to the wide path straight ahead.

2 Take the left detour for a few yards to see the ruins of St Margaret's church. Returning to the route follow the wide track until it enters a field. Keep straight ahead, picking up waymarks occasionally as you pass through several gates and into woodland. Pass through a gate into scrub and soon exit via a small gate into Hagg Wood. From the wood go into a field, then head for a bridge into another field opposite.

3 Keep to the right, following the line of the fence round to the right. This is Farwath, and the railway buildings opposite are the home of a besom broom maker. The North Yorkshire Moors Railway runs alongside now but the path leaves it as it passes through meadows and gates into the forest. The path leaves the forest on the left, when you go through a gate onto a wide track. Follow this round to the right then in a few yards climb diagonally upwards to the right.

4 Where the path crosses a wider track bear left onto it and follow it to the road. At the road go left, then keep on it all the way to Levisham Station. Cross the line carefully and take the forest road straight ahead for about 1 mile. Look for a yellow waymark on the right over a bridge. Cross the railway line and follow the footpath which is signed up the hill.

5 Half way up the hill turn left and follow the path to the top of the hill. The path is undefined now, but head over the moor to the forest plantation on the left. Keeping the trees on the left follow them for a couple of hundred yards, then turn right over the moor past a prominent stone until you reach a wide, well-defined track.

6 Join the track to the left and on the horizon you will see the ruins of Skelton Tower. The view from the tower over Newtondale is stunning, and if you are fortunate you might see a steam train puffing along the dale. Retrace your steps from the tower, cross the track that you came on and head for the path up the opposite hillside. Once over the crest of the hill follow the path as far as a stone wall.

7 Turn left and head downhill to arrive at Dundale Pond. Leave the pond by the track up the hill on the right signposted to Levisham Braygate. Follow the track over the moor to a gate in the corner of a field and leave by the stone stile into a muddy lane. This eventually meets a road which takes you back to Levisham village. If you came by train, turn right where the lane meets the road and continue along to Levisham Station.

FACT FILE

Distance 8½ miles
Time 3 hours
Maps OS Landranger 94 or 100, OS Outdoor Leisure 27
Start/parking Levisham, grid ref 833905. Please park sensibly
Terrain Firm paths but first section can be extremely boggy if wet
Nearest town Pickering
Refreshments Levisham, The Horse Shoe Inn. Recommended for good ale and food

Public transport The North Yorkshire Moors Railway runs all year round between Pickering and Grosmont, stopping at Levisham station. Tel 01751 472508 for details
Stiles A couple of easy ones
Suitable for Children and dogs

ALONG THE WAY

Levisham is a pretty moorland village with the Horseshoe Inn as its centrepiece. It is the start of the walk to Skelton Tower which gives glimpses of some of the most majestic scenery on the North York Moors. Stunning Newtondale was gouged out by water escaping from Eskdale at the end of the last ice age.

In 1836 George Stephenson opened a railway along Newtondale, although the coaches were initially drawn by horses. The railway was in operation for over 100 years until it closed in the Beeching era. It was reopened as the North Yorkshire Moors Railway some years later.

BEAUTY AND MISERY

Walk from Hackness, with its religious connections, to an ancient inn at Langdale End, taking in the strangely named Mount Misery.

1 Start near the bridge over Low Dales Beck, adjacent to the Silpho junction. Walk past the school, post office and church towards the Hall. After passing under a fine bridge look for the ice-house in the wood on the left. Continue along the road until you arrive at a group of public footpath signs. Take the one on the right to do a U-turn and walk along a shady path through the trees, keeping close to the fence on your left.

2 This path leads to a stile into a meadow - follow the waymarks across the grass as you pass behind the Hall and lake. Eventually you come to a stile in the middle of a fence crossing the field. Follow the waymarks behind Mill Farm, then drop down to the road, crossing a stile in the hedge. Cross the road diagonally left then turn right at the footpath sign. Take the bridge over the River Derwent and into a field leading to Wrench Green.

3 Keep straight ahead to join a Tarmac road, then carry on up the hill, following the sign for Cockmoor Hall. At the entrance to Slack Farm follow the footpath sign along the farm road. In a few hundred yards go right at the waymark up the hill. Keep following these waymarks round to the left, then into a copse of trees where you go right. At the end of the trees continue through the gorse bushes and over the hill, bearing slightly left.

4 Look out for the next waymark and a stile, then go down the hill and right through a small gate, following the yellow arrow. Go through the trees and you soon emerge at the farm. This high ground is called Mount Misery and offers good views across to Troutsdale. Keeping the farm on your left, follow the fence past the farm buildings and head straight on.

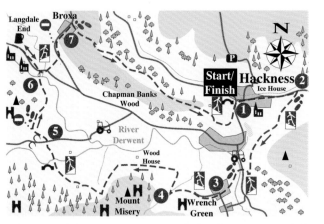

Cross a stile in the hedge opposite, then make your way down an overgrown path and onto a farm road. Turn right and follow it until you reach the tarmac road.

5 Take the public bridleway opposite and climb the hill on a wide track. The route splits at a small gate. Keep right here along the edge of the field, following the waymark. The path soon crosses a stile into a field, then heads diagonally right to another stile in the hedge. Bear left over the stile and head down through the bracken, eventually reaching a stone bridge on the right.

6 Cross the bridge, then walk past the farm to the road. Turn left here and go up the hill if you want to take some refreshment at the Moorcock Inn. Then retrace your steps to the farm, past the church, to follow the road to a bridge over the River Derwent. Immediately after the bridge cross a stile that takes you into a field on the left. You turn immediately right and go straight up the bank side on a sometimes undefined path. Half-way up you meet a wide bridleway - turn left onto it and continue to the top of the hill, where you emerge onto the road through a gate.

7 Go left into Broxa. At the end of the village, where the road narrows, follow the footpath sign to the right along a wide track. In a few yards keep straight ahead and cross the stile into the field. Follow the track and its waymarks over several stiles and fields. After five stiles and a fence you are nearing the end of this peninsula of land. Keep to the right near the trees now and look for an obvious wide track leading through a gate downhill. At the road turn left to return to your car.

FACT FILE

Distance 7 miles
Time 3 hours
Map OS Landranger 101, OS Outdoor Leisure 27
Start Hackness, grid ref 968906
Terrain Easy field paths and farm tracks
Nearest town Scarborough
Parking Roadside near the Silpho road junction

Refreshments The Moorcock Inn at Langdale End
Public transport Countryside Bus Services run to Hackness on Thursdays and Saturdays, tel 01723 870790
Stiles Numerous, some poorly maintained, one difficult
Suitable for Children; dogs on leads through stock fields

ALONG THE WAY

One of the oldest ale houses in the area is at Langdale End. The Moorcock Inn has recently been sympathetically refurbished and retains a great deal of its old charm. The beer and sandwiches are recommended.
Hackness village has religious connections with St Hilda of Whitby Abbey. Don't forget to visit the church to see the old inscriptions and stone relics.

Start your walk in the picturesque village of Hackness – make sure you allow time to visit the fascinating church

The moors of Black Fell in Lancashire, looking north to Ingleborough and Whernside on the horizon

NORTH WEST

ON THE WATERFRONT

This walk takes in two canals and one of the finest surviving Jacobean buildings in the country. Drink in the fine views and the wealth of history that this pleasant part of Cheshire has to offer.

1 Leave Acton heading back towards Nantwich for a few yards. On the right is a footpath sign to Marsh Lane – follow this, heading past Dorfold Dairy Farm.

2 When you reach the metalled surface turn right along a virtually unused narrow country lane. This is known as Dig Lane and leads to a wider road – when you arrive at this, continue straight across.

3 At the next junction, a track continues straight ahead. After 500yds, past End House, turn sharp right and go through a gate. After about 50yds, pass through the gate on the left into another field and 150yds further along is canal bridge number 10. Turn right along the towpath.

4 Walk alongside the Llangollen Canal, the most popular canal in the country with boaters.

5 Four Hurleston locks indicate the end of the Llangollen Canal. This is a boat bottleneck, with plenty of action.

6 The towpath is on the opposite side of the Shropshire Union canal. Cross the bridge and turn right, then follow the towpath.

7 The canal passes over a high embankment. When the path turns sharp right, take the flight of steps that leads down to the road.

8 Turn right and pass under the aqueduct, following the road back to Acton. The aqueduct was built by the canal's engineer Thomas Telford and is an elegant cast iron structure. He was an early proponent of metal for bridging and used it to wonderful effect for the first time in 1805 on the Llangollen Canal.

9 Walk past Dorfold Hall and, if time allows, stop here for a visit. Afterwards, follow the road round to the centre of Acton, allowing time to explore St Mary's church. It was built in 1180 and much of the original building remains.

FACT FILE

Distance 7½ miles
Time 4 hours
Map OS Landranger 118
Start The Star Inn, Acton on A534 Nantwich to Wrexham road
Terrain Level, easy walking
Nearest town Nantwich
Parking Ample street parking close to pub and a new car park opposite
Refreshments The Star Inn in Acton. A shop at Burland sells almost everything
Public transport Midland Red service 84 Hanley to Chester. Tel 01270 505350
Stiles One
Suitable for Children

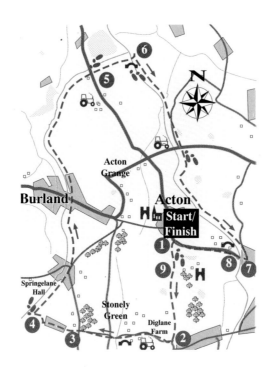

ALONG THE WAY

The Llangollen Canal was opened in the early 19th century and was lucky to escape closure in 1944 when the owners, the LMS Railway Company, abandoned huge lengths of canal in this area. It managed to survive because it had become an open water supply, from the river Dee in Wales, to the reservoir by the Hurleston locks.

After your walk, spare a little time to visit Nantwich. It's full of character and has many half-timbered buildings, some of which are more than 400 years old.

Dorfold Hall was built in 1616 for Ralph Wilbraham and is one of the best surviving Jacobean buildings in the country. Still privately owned, it played a significant part in the six-week Siege of Nantwich during the Civil War, when Royalists laid siege after the town declared itself to be on the side of Parliament.

BOWLAND'S BEST CRAGS

Clougha isn't the highest fell in Bowland but it is undoubtedly the finest, having superb sculpted crags. This walk is best appreciated at a leisurely pace.

1 From the gate at the back of Rigg Lane car park follow the grassy track, taking right forks at the next two junctions. At a wall corner leave the track (now private) and turn left over the stile. Continue on duckboards across wetlands. The path now climbs by a stream through lovely oakwoods with the crags and boulders of Windy Clough to the left.

2 Take the right of two tall ladder stiles at the edge of the moors. The path now climbs to the right of the wall and veers right as the wall changes direction. It then climbs on the lower flanks of the fell before heading east across fields of heather towards the broken cliffs of Clougha Scar. At the top of the cliffs turn right towards the sleek escarpment of Clougha Pike and continue along the gritstone slabs for the summit, which is marked by two stone shelters and a trig point.

3 From the summit descend westwards on a clear path above the upper combe of Rowton Brook. Don't confuse this with the prominent rocky ramp that descends south across Rowton Brook Fell. The path begins to climb once more, with the tall stone cairn on Grit Fell, known as the Shooters Pile, clear on the horizon.

4 Watch out for a divergence of tracks at grid ref 553594 by some scattered cairns. A few yellow-topped marker posts line our return route, which heads north through the heather, crossing a new shooters' track, not yet marked on the map. The path becomes an interesting sunken track descending Black Fell to Conder Head. The plains of Lancaster and the Lune Valley are now spread beneath your feet, beyond the gritstone outcrops of Caton Moor.

5 Descend a steep grassy slope into a deep clough and turn left to follow a track beneath the edge. The track becomes quite distinct as it climbs out of the clough to the left of some woodland onto the moors. It continues west above Cragg Wood with fine gritstone tors jutting out from the heather. Rejoin the new shooters' track and this time follow it down the hillside through a five-bar gate and onwards to another gate at the edge of the access area near a large house.

6 Don't go through the gate this time, but turn left along a grassy track that roughly follows the wall. It passes through scrubland and crosses a deep clough via a tall footbridge before it meets the outward track at grid ref 528604. Turn right along the track back to the car park.

NOTE: Walkers looking to extend this short route can follow the clear track along the ridge to Grit Fell (or even Ward's Stone) before retracing their steps. Its extra height makes it a good viewpoint although the summit itself is dull.

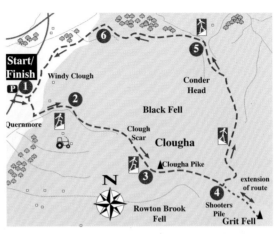

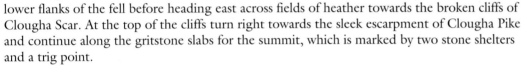

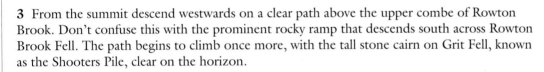

FACT FILE

Distance 5 miles or 7 miles (extended to Grit Fell)
Time 3–4 hours
Maps OS Landranger 102 and 97
Start/parking Rigg Lane car park, grid ref 526605
Nearest town Lancaster
Terrain Moorland tracks. The route uses the Clough Access Area but is not a right of way. It crosses active grouse moors and certain restrictions apply. No dogs, no camping and no fires. It can be closed on up to 12 days a year between August 12 and December 12 but never on Sundays. For further information contact Tourist Information, tel 01200 25566.
Refreshments None on route
Public transport None available
Stiles Several on the ridge, including both ladder and step stiles
Not suitable for Dogs and the disabled. Walkers should be equipped with good boots and map-reading skills.

ALONG THE WAY

Clougha's summit views are extensive and include the sweep of Morecambe Bay from the Fylde Coast to the Lakeland peaks. In the other direction, across vast tracts of crag-studded heather, are the Three Peaks of Yorkshire and Ward's Stone, Bowland's highest hill.

Jenny Brown's Point is just south of Silverdale

ALONG THE WAY

The Silverdale peninsula nestles under the shadow of the Lake District and is dotted with nature reserves. Early on you pass through a large area of limestone pavement called Gait Barrows. Home to numerous rare limestone-loving plants, the area is closed except along the footpath to all but permit holders.

FACT FILE

Distance 10 miles
Time 4 hours
Map OS Landranger 97
Start/parking Layby, grid ref 494761
Terrain Mostly distinct paths and a small amount of country lanes. Some stretches are very muddy
Nearest town Silverdale
Refreshments Numerous in Silverdale

Public transport None
Stiles Numerous
Suitable for All, but supervise young children on Jack Scout due to close proximity of cliffs

LIMESTONE LANDSCAPE

This walk takes you over a wide variety of landscapes, ranging from rare limestone pavement to flat seamarsh.

1 Leaving the layby, return to the junction and take the public footpath right. Go through the five-barred gate and at the top of the climb take the right-hand fork. Where the track veers right continue straight ahead along the grassy path alongside the drystone wall. Pass through the next gate and take the path to the left. Go through the squeezer stile and continue along the field track over Gait Barrows. Climb the ladder stile and walk to the gateway, ignoring a ladder stile to the right. Walk through the next field, a gate, then up the track through the squeezer stile.

2 At the road turn left and continue, passing Hawes Water on the left. Just after Challon Hall turn left and follow the footpath signed to Silverdale. Head for the gateway in the far right corner. Take the right of the two gates and follow the track through the hedge and across the second field. Cross the railway and field to the lane. Turn right and at the next road junction left. Go left down The Row and as the road begins to climb take the footpath to the right signed for the church.

3 Go through the white kissing gate and carry on to the church. Pass through a gap stile and then go left towards the gateway. At the road turn right and then left onto the field track. Walk alongside the wall on your left, towards the church. Go through the kissing gate and continue with the wall to your right. Climb the next squeezer stile and walk along the path before turning right towards Emesgate Lane. Turn right onto the lane and then left along a footpath to Cove Road. Turn left along the road and continue to the left-hand fork, signed The Shore. Walk through the kissing gate, keeping close to the wall on your left. Go through a kissing gate, up the slope to the next gate and continue over fields of Bank House Farm. Head for the far left corner of the field and go through another kissing gate.

4 At the road turn right and then immediately left at the fork signed Gibralter. Continue ahead, passing Woodwell Lane and at the road junction walk right, keeping parallel with the coast as you head for Jenny Brown's Point. At the sign for Jack Scout go through the gate on the right and continue with the sea on the right. All paths lead back to the road, where you continue. Before the farm at the end of the road veer right onto a stony beach and walk on, heading for the old chimney. Walk to the distant stile, then to a signpost. Turn right, making for Crag Foot.

5 Climb two stiles, then head right through a gate, left under the railway and right along the road. At the next old chimney turn left and then after 100yds take the footpath right. Take the next footpath left and follow a track through woods to the farm track. Go through the gateway and over fields. Walk through the next gateway and along the footpath signed 'straight ahead'. Take the left fork, climb the stile at the gateway and bear right across a field. Walk close to the left of a huge oak tree, then up into new woodland and over a squeezer stile. Go across the next fields. Keeping the wall to your left, walk through the gateway and along the track.

6 Turn left at the road to pass the entrance of Leighton Hall. When you arrive at the brow of the hill take the footpath on the left. Follow the path to a viewpoint, then strike downhill towards Leighton Hall, taking the gate to the right of the hall entrance. Follow the road past the rear of Leighton Hall and then go through the gate on the right. Follow the farm track through fields in the direction of the distant limestone pavement. Ignoring the gate to the left that leads to farm buildings, press on ahead to the road and then bear left to return to the start.

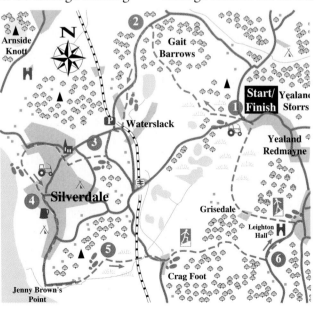

SANDSTONE STROLL

This easy route through forestry and over open pasture is ideal for a family, although care must be taken at the small stretch where the path ventures along the top of a wall.

1 Leave the park and enter Primrose Wood by the Forestry Commission road. Here, walk ahead into the woods, ignoring the path to the left, signed Sandstone Trail. Continue to the very bottom of the dip and take the short track on the right, indicated by a yellow circle with a boot. At the T-junction of paths turn left and walk along the edge of the woods for a short distance. Just before the top of the incline turn right up the flight of steps and cross the stile into the field. Walk straight up the field with the hedge to your right, pass through the next kissing gate and continue in the same direction, now with the hedge to your left. Cross the next stile and walk along the narrow footpath between two hedges.

2 When you reach the country lane bear left and then soon after go right down a track signed Sandstone Trail. Parts of this path are extremely muddy due to horse riding. At the bottom of the path turn left and walk on to where the lane veers left. At this point cross the stile to the right and continue straight ahead, with the hedge to the right, until you cross the stile at the end of the field. Bear left here and walk along the top of the field, then turn right down the farm track.

3 Walk down the hill, climbing two stiles on the way. When you reach the bottom corner of the field, walk right along the stream until you reach a footbridge. Cross the bridge and press on in the same direction – follow the perimeter of the field until a stile leads you onto a country lane. Turn right and

go straight ahead at the first crossroads, then turn right at the next one. Turn right again at the next T-junction.

4 Just after passing Ivy Cottage on the left, continue ahead through the gate and along the green lane. At the end of the green lane take care of the deceptively deep slurry covering the path near the gates. It is possible to pick your way around the right-hand side. Walk through the gate ahead, then take the aluminium gate on the right and continue with the hedge on your left. Walk around the field perimeter until you reach a huge ash tree with a fence constructed from half-round timbers. Climb the fence and carry on, keeping towards the left of the field. Walk along the concrete track that leads to Home Farm. Pass through two sets of double gates, taking care to close the gates behind you. Take the track on the left and leave the farm to emerge onto a lane.

5 Head left down the lane, then go right at the staggered crossroads. This takes you up Chapel Lane and then you turn left into Gooseberry Lane through the cottages. When you reach a concrete private road take the footpath that goes immediately to the right of a holly hedge. This runs along the top of a wall and care needs to be taken. Follow the path up a flight of steps and then cross a stile and bear right alongside a fence. Cross the fields, climbing more stiles and continue into the small copse. Ignoring the farm track, walk up to the road and turn right to return to the car.

FACT FILE

Distance 7 miles
Time 3 hours
Map OS Landranger 117
Start/parking Forest Gate car park on Waste Lane, grid ref 536678
Terrain Mostly distinct paths and a small amount of country lanes. Some muddy stretches
Nearest town Chester
Refreshments Th'ouse at Top, Waste Lane
Public transport None
Stiles Numerous
Suitable for Children

ALONG THE WAY

The first part of the route follows the popular Sandstone Trail, a route devised, managed and maintained by Cheshire County Council. Opened in stages from 1975, the route is 30 miles long and closely follows the sandstone ridge that dominates the countryside of central Cheshire. Some of the most imposing views of the Cheshire flatlands can be enjoyed from this route and there are fantastic views of Beeston Castle.

SECRETS REVEALED

Garstang, sandwiched between the wide plains of the Fylde and the heather hills of Bowland, is the centre for many a good walk. This one wanders through woodland and over high plains and visits a little-known castle.

1 The walk begins on the towpath of the Lancaster Canal just past St Thomas's church. You get onto it at the far side of the road bridge next to the Owd Tithebarne, a popular bar-restaurant. Pass a large berthing area, usually decorated by colourful boats, and then head east past a new housing estate. You will soon find yourself walking alongside open fields. As the canal passes under the Catterall road, the ruins of Greenhalgh Castle appear from behind the trees, and the hills of western Bowland peep over rolling farmland.

2 At bridge number 56 you leave the towpath. Climb the steps and cross the bridge. A cart track leads across fields and onto bridges across the London to Glasgow railway and the M6 motorway. Veer left through the farmyard of Turners Farm (grid ref 510449, not named on Landranger maps) and follow the drive to the road. Turn right and then make two left turns along pleasant tree-lined lanes.

3 At Sullom Side, a rutted cart track guides you to the top of the hill. Here you can look down on Calder Vale. Go through the left of the two gates and follow the wire fence on the right downhill to a gate at the edge of the woods. The path beyond, which can be a little overgrown in high summer, meets a stony track that runs all the way along the valley bottom. Across the river, you should be able to make out a row of terraced cottages through the trees.

4 The track emerges at the roadside just above Calder Vale. You could take a break here to explore the village, but to continue along the route, follow some stone steps up the grassy bank opposite. A narrow shrub-lined lane takes you behind some houses and the path, now waymarked, continues across two fields which have stiles at the boundaries. Cross the primitive footbridge to pass to the right of a white cottage (grid ref 528457). Soon afterwards a wooden stile on the right leads onto a grassy track past another cottage to the roadside.

5 Cross the road and climb a small stile, then head across fields by a fence and line of trees. At the top of the hill there are spectacular views over the fields of the Fylde, gradually fading to the outlines of the Lancashire coast. When you've taken it all in, make your way down towards Heald Farm. Watch out for a stile to the right just before the farmyard. This marks the start of a path that heads west through the trees to meet a concrete farm track leading to the road.

6 At grid ref 514457 follow an unclassified road past New Hall Farm and over the M6 and railway. Just beyond, leave the road and join a path to the right, which heads across fields and an old railway cutting. The well-defined path then meets a dirt track leading past Greenhalgh Castle Farm and close by the ruined castle, which was built in 1490 for the Earl of Derby. The track becomes a road and leads into Garstang. Turn right at the junction with the main road which heads back towards the town centre.

FACT FILE

Distance 7 miles
Time 3½ hours
Maps OS Landranger 102, OS Pathfinder 668
Start Lancaster Canal by Owd Tithebarne, Garstang, grid ref 489450
Terrain Field paths, country lanes and farm tracks
Nearest town Preston
Parking Large free car park in the centre of Garstang
Refreshments None on route. A variety of pubs in Garstang
Public transport Stage Coach Ribble bus services from Lancaster or Preston, tel 01524 424555
Stiles Numerous, mostly simple wooden step stiles
Suitable for Most walkers, provided that they can negotiate simple stiles. Dogs should be on leads

ALONG THE WAY

Calder Vale is something of an enigma. Secretively sited in a wooded glen at the end of a rural cul-de-sac, its seclusion from the rest of England is both geographical and cultural. The village was founded and planned by the Quaker Jackson family, and it still has no pub. Its cottages are clustered around a huge stone-built mill, which is still working today.

Lose Hill, near Castledon, in the Peak District

EAST MIDLANDS

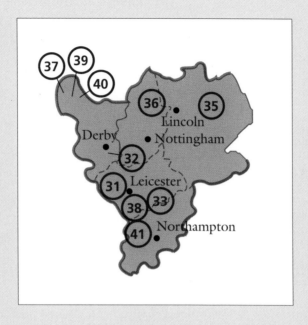

ANCIENT AND MODERN

Journey through the delightful undulating countryside of north west Leicestershire, where the new National Forest will have its roots, and explore three ancient villages.

1 With the church on your right walk along Main Street to the B5326 road and cross to School Lane opposite. Just after Home Farm the road gives way to a farm lane and in ¼ mile turn right at a horseshoe sign to join a track. Bear left through a wooden gate and continue along the track, which may be muddy, to Normanton Wood.

2 Skirt to the left of the ancient wood, then bear left at the next junction to reach a small pond on your right. Continue in the same direction, now following a woodland track, to a triangle of tracks. Bear left onto the concrete track for a short time, then rejoin the track that you were on before. Pass through a metal gate at Hill Farm where the farm road extends for 1 mile towards Packington village.

3 Turn right onto Normanton Road, then left into the village to reach the Bull and Lion pub. Cross the road bridge over the Gilwiskaw Brook and then turn left at Babelake Street, admiring a beautiful thatched cottage to your right. Go along this road out of the village – there are some splendid views of open countryside to your left and right. Ignore the track to Stonehouse Farm on the left, and you eventually arrive at a public footpath signpost where the lane bears right.

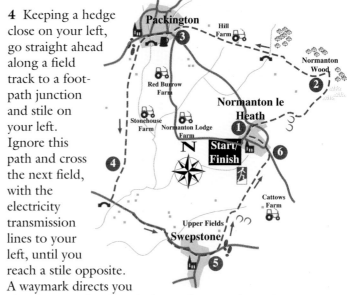

4 Keeping a hedge close on your left, go straight ahead along a field track to a footpath junction and stile on your left. Ignore this path and cross the next field, with the electricity transmission lines to your left, until you reach a stile opposite. A waymark directs you ahead to a surfaced track alongside a new bungalow. Turn right over the cattle grid and follow the access road to Stanhope House and the road. Turn left and walk along the wide grassy verge for 1 mile to Swepstone village. Ahead of you stands Swepstone church and about 200yds past Church Street turn left at a horseshoe sign by The Cottage.

5 A farm lane leads to Upper Fields Farm and by a white 'footpath only' sign join a field perimeter path. At the next marker post, turn right and continue along the field-edge path, eventually crossing into the next field. The path climbs a hill and widens out before reaching Heather Lane.

6 Turn left along the road into Normanton Le Heath and at the road junction with The Hollow climb a stile. Continue towards the church, descending a grassy field to a stream, then climb to a stile adjacent to the church. A short path passes through the churchyard and brings you to a gate on Main Street and back to the start.

FACT FILE

Distance 8 miles
Time 3 hours
Maps OS Landranger 128, OS Pathfinder 873
Start Holy Trinity Church, Normanton Le Heath, grid ref 378128
Terrain Country tracks and lanes. No steep hills
Nearest town Ashby de la Zouch

Parking Street parking around the church
Refreshments Bull and Lion in Packington
Public transport Tel Busline 0116 251 1411
Stiles Very few
Suitable for Children and dogs

ALONG THE WAY

Normanton Le Heath derives its name from a settlement of Northmen (Norwegians) and the open heath was enclosed in 1629. Normanton Wood is one of the few remaining ancient woodlands in this area and has a wonderful display of bluebells in spring. Swepstone village overlooks the Mease Valley.

CASTLE COUNTRY

This timeless walk explores Elvaston Castle Country Park then traces part of the disused Derby Canal.

1 Opposite the church gates take the woodland path to a park service road, then turn right to the riding school. Head left along the track through the country park to reach the B5010 road and turn left. Cross the River Derwent and turn right at a public footpath sign over the railway bridge.

2 Descend the steps where a wooded path runs adjacent to the railway line. This is the disused Derby canal – it was closed in 1961, but pockets of water still linger to the left of the path. Cross a footbridge, then two stiles in quick succession, to a farm track. Continue ahead, following the waymarks. A line of stiles takes you over Draycott Fields to the A6005 road. Walk beneath the road bridge onto a wide grassy track; this soon swings to the left before returning to a conventional field perimeter path.

3 Turn left along the road for 300yds to an obvious opening on the left just past Draycott Fields Farm. Make your way to a group of trees and pass to the left of them where an obvious field path leads to a wooden footbridge. Cross the next field in the same direction to a track and turn right to reach the B5010 road again. Turn right along Nottingham Road to Lodge House and turn left.

4 Follow the obvious path ahead through Hopwell Hall Grounds for ½ mile then turn left along a well-used field footpath heading towards Ockbrook. Climb a stile on the brow of a hill and then descend to another one in the left corner of the field. Here, follow a thin path through untidy woodland before emerging onto the road. Turn right into the pretty village of Ockbrook and

after the White Swan turn left to a road junction.

5 Walk past the Queens Head pub for ¼ mile to a public footpath sign and track. Cross three fields, heading towards Spondon, then turn left where the paths intersect and make for the A52. Cross the dual carriageway to the stile opposite and follow the field path to a footbridge. Cross this onto a rough track to the A6005 in Borrowash.

6 Go along an alleyway onto a track that takes you to the disused Derby Canal and bridge. Turn left along the old canal bed onto a well-used footpath by the railway line; in due course the footpath rises and is a good vantage point. Turn right along the B5010 and retrace your footsteps along the road to the main entrance of Elvaston Castle Country Park.

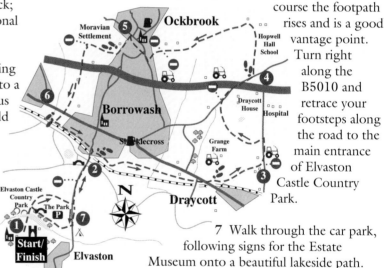

7 Walk through the car park, following signs for the Estate Museum onto a beautiful lakeside path. Turn left along the track to the castle courtyard; the entrance to the church is signposted to the right.

FACT FILE

Distance 8¼ miles
Time 3 hours
Maps OS Landranger 129, OS Pathfinder 833
Start St Bartholomew church, Elvaston, grid ref 406330
Terrain Flat walking along good footpaths, bridleways and tracks
Nearest town Derby
Parking Small area around church or country park car park, charging 60p in the week or £1.20 at weekends
Refreshments The White Swan or The Queens Head, Ockbrook
Public transport Barton Buses from Derby or Nottingham. Tel

Busline 01332 292200 for details
Stiles Many wooden ones, some enclosed
Suitable For Children and small dogs

ALONG THE WAY

Elvaston Castle Country Park is well worth a visit. The Castle was once the home of the Earls of Harrington and was built in the early 19th century. The castle is not open to the public but the magnificent gardens are. Look out for the beautiful and colourful Golden Gates. The church is not part of the country park and is currently being restored. All Saints church in Ockbrook has a 12th century tower and the village is one of South Derbyshire's finest.

TASTE OF THE MIDSHIRES

Sample part of the Leicestershire section of the Midshires Way. This area is rich in tradition with small villages, country halls, churches and public houses which are a delight to explore.

1 Walk along Main Street, passing the Black Horse on your left, to reach the end of the village and a public bridleway signpost by the tennis courts. Go through a gate onto a farm track, then walk ahead on the obvious field path for ¾ mile, keeping a hedge to your right. Bear left over a footbridge and make for a wooden stump where a field perimeter path leads towards a wood. Skirt the wood to the right to reach a gate and public bridleway signpost. Turn right along the track to Rolleston, passing the Hall and church.

2 At the road junction turn left and pass the Old Stables. Follow the tree-lined parkland road almost to the B6047, then turn left onto another parkland road to a gate. Continue along this quiet byway for ¾ mile to a road junction, passing a trig point.

3 Walk into Noseley and in ¼ mile turn right at a public bridleway sign and pass through a blue gate. A path now leads through two more blue gates onto a track. Where the track bears right, join a grassy field path to reach a gate and turn l eft. As you follow the perimeter field edge there is a fine view of the Hall to your left. Go through a small wood, bear right to a field and then make for a tree opposite before descending to a stream. Cross the footbridge, climb a hill to a handmade footpath sign and head for a gate beneath the electricity transmission lines. Keep these to your right – there is no obvious path to follow, but walk slightly to the left over the next four fields to reach Moat Farm at Glooston.

4 Turn left, passing the Old Barn Inn, to the road junction and join the road signposted to Cranoe. Walk along the quiet road for 1 mile, climbing slowly to a Midshires Way sign on the left above the village.

5 An uphill path leads to a gate. Keeping a hedge to your left, follow the field path ahead for ½ mile to a gate and marker post. A long field path brings you to the next gate and a wide field edge path leads to a track.

6 In 50yds turn right for Tugby, following the field perimeter path, then track, passing Keythorpe Lodge Farm to the left. Join the farm access road for ¾ mile, passing a second trig point, to reach the road by Keythorpe Hall Farm.

7 Cross to the road opposite and follow it for about 1 mile to Tugby.

FACT FILE

Distance 10 miles
Time 4 hours
Maps OS Landranger 141, OS Pathfinders 895 and 916
Start The Green, Tugby, grid ref 762009
Terrain Undulating. Good bridleways and footpaths with some road walking along quiet byways or country lanes

Nearest town Leicester
Parking Roadside by village stores and pub
Refreshments Two pubs in Tugby.
Public transport Midland Fox operates Leicester-Peterborough service. Phone Busline on 0116 2 511411
Stiles Easy, in good condition
Suitable for Older children and dogs

ALONG THE WAY

The Midshires Way is a new long-distance bridleway and footpath that crosses Central England, linking the Ridgeway with the Trans-Pennine trail, and then the Pennine Way.
Both Rolleston and Noseley are fascinating hamlets with splendid country houses lying in secluded parkland. The houses are private but you can walk through the parkland. If you like to visit churches, don't miss the quaint church at Rolleston.

Picturesque Rollington Lake is seen just before you reach point 2

ESTATE SECRETS

Explore some of the more out-of-the-way parts of the Chatsworth estate using a series of concessionary paths.

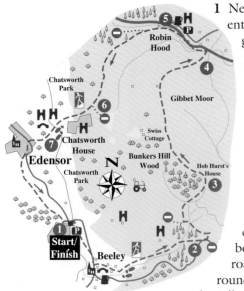

1 Near the entrance to the garden centre, a path drops to the road bridge that takes you across the River Derwent. The signed path on the right leads across the field to the hamlet of Beeley. Walk through the churchyard, then bear right at the road. Follow it round to the left and up the valley. The lane degenerates to a track. Where it turns off to the right, follow the grass path straight on, walking past a gate with a double stile. At another gate, the path enters the wood. Climbing steadily, cross the stream and negotiate a wet section, then bear right. Watch out for a sharp turn back to the left at a junction, then in a grassy area bear right to reach a stile in the wall at the top of the hill. Most of the climbing has now been done.

2 Follow the track to the left and round the left-hand bend. Cross the stile beside the gate at the next left bend, then turn immediately right off the track, following a clear path marked with white arrows across the moor. Bear right to a high stile beside the wood, then follow the wall. When you reach an 'open country' sign, Hob Hurst's House is just along the path to the right.

3 Continue parallel with the wall along clearly marked vehicle tracks for well over 1 mile. When the wall turns left, continue along the track.

4 At a watercourse a sign indicates a waymarked path on the left that drops into a valley and follows the stream. Later waymarks direct you onto higher ground above the stream – cross a stile, then follow a fence on your right.

5 Go ahead to a ladder stile, climb this and bear half-left. Follow the fence and the waymarks, with some steep drops on the right. The rough path leads through bracken and some stiles into a field and then over a high stile in a wall. Follow the wall uphill then to a stile into the wood. Go immediately left then right along the track until you can turn right beside a tall building (the Hunting Tower).

6 You can follow the track as it zigzags downhill but alternatively, just below the Hunting Tower look for a path on the right which leads down some steps. Approaching another track, bear left across the stream, then cross the track and follow the path down to a metalled track. This comes into the parkland beside the stables, with Chatsworth House below. Go straight downhill to the bridge over the river. Over the bridge to the right there are fine views of Chatsworth House.

7 Across the bridge, you can turn left anywhere and use the river or road to guide you to the car park. However, it is worth following the gravel path over the rise to Edensor village, before making your way across the parkland to the car. Keep well above the road for the best views of the house.

ALONG THE WAY

Hob Hurst's House has an intriguing name, but not much to see. It is a neolithic earthwork and there is an explanatory plaque at the site. The conduit at point 4 takes water to the Emperor Lake in the woods above Chatsworth. This feeds the fountain in the gardens. Much of Chatsworth parkland is open to the public. In the quieter areas you will almost certainly see deer. Edensor village was moved to its present site when the park was landscaped by Capability Brown.

FACT FILE

Distance 9½ miles
Time 5 hours
Maps OS Landranger 119, OS Outdoor Leisure 24
Start/parking Calton Lees car park on the B6012 Baslow–Rowsley road, at the south end of Chatsworth park, grid ref 259685.
Terrain Paths, tracks and grassland. One rough section. From Hob Hurst's House the path is good, but may be exposed in bad weather.
Nearest town Bakewell

Refreshments At the garden centre at the start. Also the Robin Hood pub 10 minutes from point 5
Public transport Weekday buses Matlock to Baslow. Tel 01246 250450
Stiles About a dozen
Suitable for Older children and dogs on leads

St Peter's church in Edensor, near the end of the walk

RED HILL CONTRASTS

Walk through the countryside around Red Hill, a naturalists' paradise with splashes of colour from its soils, once iron-rich mud formed over 100 million years ago.

1 From the turn-off at Scamblesby take the short path on the left to the A153 just by the school at the road junction. Cross this and continue over fields, following a stream and then a small fishing lake until you reach a white painted bridge.

2 Ignoring all other waymarkers turn right on the road passing Asterby until you reach a junction signposted to the left to Goulceby. Take the footpath on the right, climbing gently to Red Hill Nature Reserve. The red chalk here is rich in fossils and many can be found in the loose soil. Descend by the road to Manor Farm and take the path through the farmyard. (Beware of the dog, but it is chained!) Continue until you pass through the old cemetery in Goulceby and then turn left down a metalled track. Cross the next road and go ahead over a stile to Goulceby. Note the undulations in the last field by the large fallen tree. This is evidence of the medieval village that stood here.

3 Emerge into the village and turn right at the road. The Three Horseshoes pub is on the corner. Carry on along the road, passing the post office and, where the road bends to the left, continue straight ahead at the no through road sign. Pass the waymarker on the left but take the right-hand bend and follow the next waymarker to the left and eventually back to the white painted bridge that you first encountered at point 2. Turn right along the road and then left across the field to the A153. Turn right and, just before the bend near some houses take the trail on the left. Continue straight ahead at the metalled waymarker in the fields and climb steadily to the viewpoint over the next stile. Pause here to admire the excellent views of the Wolds. Walk down the farm track and turn left onto the road to Belchford.

4 After about ¼ mile follow Viking Way waymarkers, starting at a stile on the left. Cross the fields to return to Scamblesby, ignoring all alternative paths indicated by Countryside Commission markers along the way. The path joins a road next to a house called The Beeches and your route then continues past the post office to the T-junction next to the school, where you started.

ALONG THE WAY

Red Hill Nature Reserve has facilities for parking and picnics and offers splendid views; it is so named because of the colour of the exposed red chalk soil. The area is noted for its variety of insects, including butterflies, moths and spiders. Lizards can be seen, and it is also an inland breeding site for the meadow pipit.
Belchford was inhabited in prehistoric times and a number of flint artefacts and stone axes have been found. During the Lincolnshire Rising in 1536 Nicholas Leache, the Rector of Belchford, refused to acknowledge Henry VIII as head of the church. As a result he was hung, drawn and quartered for treason at Tyburn.

A well-earned rest in the countryside near Belchford

FACT FILE

Distance 9½ miles
Time 4 hours
Maps OS Landranger 122, OS Pathfinder 766, OS Pathfinder 748
Start Scamblesby, grid ref 276788
Terrain Well waymarked paths
Nearest towns Horncastle, Louth

Parking Scamblesby just off A153 Horncastle to Louth road
Refreshments The Three Horseshoes in Goulceby or The Blue Bell Inn, Belchford
Public transport Lincs Road Car (Weds only), tel 01522 532424; Haynes, tel 01205 722359
Stiles Numerous, well maintained

Suitable for All ages, dogs on leads, livestock in some fields

WAY TO A WINDMILL

Enjoy views from the ridge above the Trent plain and a visit to a windmill.

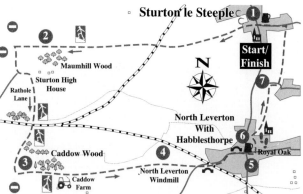

1 Park near Sturton-le-Steeple church and walk past the pond. At the crossroads go ahead along Springs Lane, where a path of stone slabs leads you past a delightful waterside garden. After about 3⁄4 mile, ignore the bridleway on the right but soon swing right under the railway bridge. There are wide verges and neat hedges on the lane leading uphill.

2 Though only 200ft high, there are extensive views, with South Wheatley to the north and Lincoln Cathedral visible to the east. Less attractive though necessary are the three power stations on the banks of the Trent. The lane curves left, but our route is ahead along the Trent Valley Way. Go through the handgate and follow the edge of two fields, using the gates provided, to Blue Stocking Lane. Turn left and follow the lane to join Whinleys Road. Turn left here for a few yards, then right into Rathole Lane.

3 At the foot of the hill, beside the level crossing, is a nature reserve in the care of the Nottinghamshire Wildlife Trust. The reserve owes its existence to the tunnel and cutting excavated for the Retford-Gainsborough railway in 1849. The spoil was piled up nearby and has developed naturally into rough woodland, rich in wild flowers. Cross the railway line, watching out for coal trains going to West Burton Power Station, and continue uphill beside woodlands. Turn left down Retford Gate, at first a grassy lane, then stone, then tarmac beyond the windmill.

4 Stop for a visit at North Leverton Mill (see Along the Way). Now called Mill Lane, our route joins a busy road, where you turn left along the pavement into North Leverton.

5 After pausing at the Royal Oak for refreshment, continue 200yds along the Littleborough Road. A signpost on the left points to the church: the path passes to the left of the church, goes through a gap behind the churchyard and crosses a grassy lane. After climbing the stile, make for the middle of the field, then turn right towards the corner, where there is another stile.

6 Walk across the grass field to a gate, then go half-left across an arable field to a stile. Cross a narrow meadow, then continue to the corner of the next field. Climb the stile and follow the edge of another grass field to a double stile and footbridge where there is a Trent Valley Way sign.

7 At this point the route has been diverted to the right around the field edge to a stile into Three Leys Lane. Turn left to another stile and keep following the right-hand boundary, watching out for rabbit holes. A small grass field brings you to the Littleborough road, where you turn left to return to your starting point and the Reindeer Inn.

FACT FILE

Distance 7 miles
Time 3½ hours
Maps OS Landranger 120, OS Pathfinder 68/78
Start Sturton-le-Steeple church, map reference 788838
Terrain Mostly on green lanes and grass paths, with a couple of gentle climbs
Nearest town Retford
Parking Near the church, or ask the landlord of the Reindeer Inn for permission to use his car park
Refreshments Royal Oak, North Leverton and Reindeer Inn, Sturton

Public transport Two-hourly services (95 and 95A) between Retford and Gainsborough. Fewer on Sundays
Stiles 12 wooden stiles
Suitable for Children and dogs

ALONG THE WAY

On your right at the top of Rathole Lane is the High Point Surge Vessel. This is connected to a pipeline through which the fuel ash from Cottam power station is pumped to Sutton-cum-Lound.
North Leverton Mill was a subscription mill, built in 1813 for and by local farmers to grind corn. Since 1956 it has been run by a limited company, grinding grain and rolling or crushing oats and barley for animal feed. It is one of only two working windmills in Nottinghamshire and is open to visitors most afternoons (not Tuesday or Saturday).

PEAK PERFORMANCE

This relatively gentle route takes you to a neat rocky peak. A canal and old transport routes add interest to the walk.

1 Cross the main road from the station and walk down Canal Street. Follow the towpath from the right-hand side of the canal wharf. Cross the bridge over the Buxworth arm, go left and continue to bridge 32.

2 Turn right, cross the river, then follow the track past a pleasant group of cottages. Under a pair of bridges, turn right below the embankment. Go through a gate and cross the field to a stile, then turn left uphill. At the top, follow the fence and wall, then pass through the right-hand gateway. The route diverges slightly left from the power lines and crosses an awkward stile. It then takes you through a gap at the left-hand end of a wall to a metal gate in the far corner. At the buildings ahead, take the track to the road. Turn right down to Buxworth basin.

3 Past the Navigation Inn, join the old trackway alongside the stream. After 1 mile, cross a lane, then another one and continue to a road just beside the bypass bridge.

4 Turn right under the bridge. Immediately past a house on the right, a path goes into a field. Follow the wall on the left uphill. Go through a gate and follow the right-hand wall to an awkward stile where it bends left. Head across the field to a white building at a farm. Straight across the lane follow a sign past the farm to a stile into a field. The next stile is in the stretch of cross-wall. Keep ahead along the wall, cross the stile and follow the fence on your right. This takes you to a stile and path to an iron gate. Bear left up the bank to a National Trust sign. Walk uphill inside the fence and head for the summit of Eccles Pike. Combs Reservoir stretches away in one direction, with Chinley Churn across the valley on the opposite side.

5 From the summit, go down to the lane and follow it to the right. Just past Top Eccles Farm, between two gates on the left, cross a stile. Bear slightly left and after another stile head for a gate beside a pair of electricity poles. Go downhill along the wall on the left (not the track) and through two gates between the buildings. Continue down to the main road at Tunstead Milton. The Rose and Crown pub is to the right.

6 Over the road a footpath takes you across the field to an awkward stile. Bear left, climb some steps to a metalled track crossing the embankment of Combs Reservoir and follow this to the right. Cross the railway to the buildings at Meveril Farm. Go through a gate beside a ladder stile, then pass two gates marked private. Turn right between two buildings to a metal gate and a track running slightly uphill. After a stile beside a gate, keep ahead along the right-hand side of a wall, then a fence, to cross a stream. Just ahead, a stile takes you over a wall; follow this downhill and continue past two stiles on a track above a house. After a short uphill section, follow the wall downhill. Cross another stile and continue in the direction of new houses to join a track. Follow the left-hand side of a ruined wall. Cross another stile onto a track. Cross the road and walk along Shallcross Mill Road. Past the Cromford Court Flats bear right along a path and through a tunnel. Continue until you have to turn left onto the main road, then carry on to the station.

FACT FILE

Distance 8 miles
Time 4 hours
Maps OS Landranger 110 and 119, OS Outdoor Leisure 1 & 24
Start Whaley Bridge railway station, grid ref 011815
Terrain Mostly paths and tracks
Nearest town Buxton
Parking Signposted opposite the station

Refreshments Cafés and pubs in Whaley Bridge. Pubs at Buxworth, Tunstead Milton and off route in Chinley
Public transport Trains Manchester-Buxton and buses Stockport–Buxton. For details of times tel 01298 23098
Stiles About 15, some awkward
Suitable for Children

ALONG THE WAY

Buxworth basin is currently being restored. The tramway route you follow carried minerals to the canal and you can still see the old stone sleepers. You finish the walk along the original trackbed of the Cromford and High Peak Railway, opened in 1830 with horse power, and running to the attractive canal basin at Whaley Bridge.

The first part of this walk takes you alongside the Cromford Canal.

ROMAN ROUND

This part of the Leicestershire Round encompasses the Fosse Way and the villages of Claybrooke Parva and Frolesworth.

1 From the Falconer Inn on the B4114 Leicester road, turn left along a lane to cross a bridge over the Soar Brook by a Leicestershire Round (LR) footpath sign. Cross the stile and keep the brook to your left while you follow the obvious path ahead. Go through the private cricket ground, then along an enclosed path to reach a footpath junction. Continue ahead to cross a track where you can see a double stile ahead. Cross the footbridge and then turn right, noting Cottage Farm to your right. Follow the waymarker arrows to reach the Fosse Way at Claybrooke Lodge Farm.

2 Turn right onto the old Roman road and immediately the metalled road gives way to a green track. Bear in mind that after heavy rain this track becomes very muddy. After ½ mile you pass Sharnford Lodge Farm and as you continue along the track you go through a number of kissing gates. Walk through a section of the track that is enclosed by overhanging trees, then ignore a track to the left. After several more kissing gates you reach an information board about the Fosse Way at High Cross.

3 Turn left along the B577 to a LR footpath sign on the right, telling you that Claybrooke Parva is 1½ miles. Walk along an obvious, well waymarked field path, over a number of fields to a one-hand footbridge. Cross to the next stile and, keeping a hedge to your right, then left, climb the hill to the village.

4 Walk through the village to the right, passing the church, until you come to a LR footpath sign to Claybrooke Magna Mill on the left. Go through the farmyard, then pass through three gates in quick succession to a field. Keep a hedge on your left and follow the field perimeter path over two fields to a handgate. Cross the next field diagonally left to a new wooden bridge at Claybrooke Mill. Walk through the mill yard, as indicated, to a field gate and cross to the road opposite.

5 A LR footpath sign to Frolesworth 1 mile shows the way. With a hedge to your right, go straight ahead, then follow the LR signs through a complicated set of fields to reach a track by Hall Farm. Descend the hill, enjoying the view of Frolesworth ahead, and follow the well-used path to the village.

6 At White Cottage, turn left, and in 100yds there is a public footpath sign. Pass through the farmyard and cross a field to a hedge gap opposite. Continue over a long field to reach a fence. After crossing the next field you reach the Fosse Way again.

7 Cross to a public footpath sign opposite and, keeping a hedge to your left, descend to a footbridge over a stream. A grassy path leads through two new wooden kissing gates and the footpath from Sharnford. Turn right and retrace your steps to the start.

FACT FILE

Distance 8½ miles
Time 3 hours
Maps OS Landranger 140, OS Pathfinder 914 and 915
Start The Falconer Inn, Sharnford, grid ref 484917
Terrain Mainly field footpaths and tracks. All very well waymarked
Nearest town Hinckley
Parking - The Falconer Inn (ask permission first)
Refreshments The Falconer Inn, Sharnford. Plough and Harrow, Frolesworth
Public transport Midland Fox operates frequent services. Phone Busline 01162 511411 for details
Stiles Many traditional wooden stiles
Suitable for Children and dogs

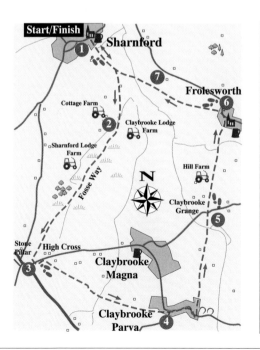

ALONG THE WAY

The Fosse Way was constructed about 45AD and was one of the principal roads of Roman Britain. It runs from Lincoln to Bath. In the hotel car park at High Cross is a stone pillar, the remains of a monument erected by the Earl of Denbigh and others in 1712. This was originally sited in the centre of Watling Street, adjacent to the Fosse Way. It was moved after lightning struck it in 1791. At Frolesworth it is worth visiting the Plough and Harrow for light refreshments.

The view from Hall Farm to the church at Frolesworth

MAKING TRACKS

Climb the prominent hill of South Head by a gentle, roundabout route with good views in all directions, passing an impressive V of railway viaducts.

South Head is a prominent feature for miles around and the walk to the summit provides excellent views

ALONG THE WAY

The railway through the Hope Valley to Chinley opened in 1894. The track that you follow near the start of the walk is the route of the older Peak Forest Tramway which ran to the canal basin at Buxworth. Inside the railway triangle beside the lane to Wash is Chinley Chapel, one of the oldest non-conformist places of worship in the area. The track past South Head is the old packhorse route from Tideswell to Hayfield.

FACT FILE

Distance 6½ miles
Time 4 hours
Maps OS Landranger 110, Outdoor Leisure 1
Start Centre of Chinley, grid ref 041825
Terrain Field paths and tracks
Nearest town Chapel-en-le-Frith
Parking Signposted off the main street
Refreshments Pub in Chinley
Public transport Buses Buxton to Whaley Bridge (not Sundays). Stopping trains Sheffield – Manchester line. For details of time tel 01298 23098
Stiles 11 or 12
Suitable for Children

1 From the start point, walk down the Whitehough road. Cross the stream, then immediately turn left towards the Dorma works. Keep to the right side of the car park to find a path along a hedge to a track. Go left, then when you have passed a pond, bear left on a path along the stream. This leads you to a bridge over a pipeline to the road. Go left, but before you reach the stream and the large building, turn right along the track to a squeezer stile beside a gate. The path takes you towards the railway viaduct ahead and then a road. Continue along the lane, then at the bypass bridge take the stile on the left and follow the field edge up the hill then on the level. South Head can be seen up to the left. Past a woodland belt, continue straight on. After a small stream, head for the houses and look for a hidden stile to the right of a two-storey house. This leads onto a lane in the small hamlet of Wash.

2 When you reach the signpost at the bottom of the hill, head across the field, keeping the stream on your left as you do so. Nearing a farm, cross the stream on a footbridge but still follow it to cross a lane. A bridge leads under the railway, then a waymark points to a hidden stile on the left. Climb half-right across the slope to gateposts. Stop for a well-earned breather here and admire the view opening out behind you, then follow the bushes to a track through Shireoaks Farm. Emerging in the open field, follow the wall uphill to a track, then turn left to its summit beside South Head.

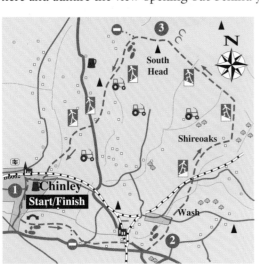

3 The top of South Head is an optional extra, but is worth the detour for the all-round view. Continue along the track. Immediately past a gate, a path over a stile on the left leads down to a track. At a fork left into a farm, keep straight on, then follow the wall to a walled track which leads to the main road. Go straight over a stile, then follow the walls downhill. In a field go half-left towards a house. Through the gate and past the left side of the house, follow the access lane to the main road and turn right to the centre of Chinley.

SHIVERING MOUNTAIN

View at close quarters the massive land slipping off the shales of Mam Tor that has destroyed the main A625 road, and contrast it with the strength of the limestone rock in which the Castleton caves have developed.

1 Across the road from Hope church, take the path on the left of the Peak Fruits shop. Go straight past the houses and continue through the squeezer stile to the left of the school. Follow stiles and field boundaries to cross the railway line. Go along the right side of the bungalow, then maintain the same direction. At a stile with two waymarks, follow the right-hand one up the hill. After two stiles, bear slightly left to find the next one, then follow the sign, still going uphill. Pass a derelict barn, then bear slightly left and follow the wall up to a high ladder stile. Go left through the gateway and walk up to the next signpost, passing Losehill Farm on your left. There are views of Mam Tor at the head of the Hope Valley. Continue on the clear path up the hill to reach a big pile of stones.

2 More energetic walkers can continue up the obvious path to Lose Hill, walk along the ridge, then descend a rough path off Back Tor. An easier route bears left, keeping level across the hillside and passing through trees. It is now worth taking the easy path along the top of the ridge to Hollins Cross, marked by its low stone pillar. Here you can admire the head of Edale with the plateau of Kinder Scout beyond.

3 Take the path that drops half-left down the hillside with the old road directly ahead. Keep left at a fork to drop to a track which you follow to the road corner. The walk up the road shows the irreparable damage due to subsidence. Turn down the access track to the Blue John Cavern.

4 Go left past a gate and ladder stile. Go straight on, past a waymark, to find a clear path over a stile which leads down around the shoulder of the hill. You are now obviously on limestone rock; you have crossed a geological boundary. The path leads to the entrance of the Treak Cliff Cavern where you can buy refreshments and there is sheltered seating. Continue for a short distance on the concrete access path, then go through a gap in the railing to follow a clear path along the hillside. This comes out just above Speedwell Cavern.

5 Just below the cavern at a National Trust sign on the right, take the path that goes round the foot of the hill. After a metal gate it becomes a lane between houses. It is worth diverting along the first turning on the right to see the impressive entrance to the Peak Cavern. Our route crosses the bridge over the stream, then bears left to follow it to the main street of Castleton.

6 Walk along the street, go round two bends and past the bus terminus. At a track on the right, follow the footpath sign for Hope.
Walk beside the stream past a water treatment works and a broken wall, then follow the fence on your right. A series of stiles now marks the route until at a hillock with trees you bear slightly left to a crossing over the railway line. More stiles show the route to a lane, where you turn left into Hope.

FACT FILE

Distance 7 miles
Time 4 hours
Maps OS Landranger 110, OS Outdoor Leisure 1
Start Hope church, grid ref 172835
Terrain Mostly field paths. A steady climb within the first 1½ miles
Nearest town Sheffield
Parking Signposted in Hope
Refreshments Cafés and pubs in Hope and Castleton
Public transport Buses from Sheffield, tel 01298 23098 for details of times. Hope railway station is well over ½ mile from the church
Stiles Lots, but mostly easy
Suitable for Older children. Stiles and sheep make it difficult for dogs

ALONG THE WAY

Blue John and Treak Cliff Caverns can be visited on foot, but Speedwell, a disused lead mine, can only be reached by boat. These caves are open throughout the winter months, but Peak Cavern is closed. In the weeks leading up to Christmas, the Castleton lights provide an added attraction for visitors as darkness falls.

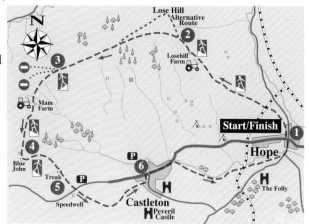

At point 2 you join the towpath and follow the Leicester line of the Grand Union Canal

HOME OF THE PLOTTERS

Visit the village where the gunpowder plot was hatched, then
enjoy a walk along the Grand Union Canal.

1 From the parish church turn left along a lane at a Jurassic Way footpath sign to reach a stile after 100yds. Join a green track which leads to a stile and field path, then bear right away from the lake to a stile on the brow of the hill. Continue ahead, passing through a copse then, keeping a hedge to your right, follow the field perimeter path eventually to reach a stream. The footpath now clings to the course of the stream until it meets the London to Birmingham railway line.

2 Take extreme care in crossing the railway tracks at the authorised point, then continue ahead with the stream on your left to the A5 road. Cross to the left of the stream and follow a thin path to Watford Locks. Go over the small bridge to the canal towpath and turn right along the Leicester Line of the Grand Union Canal. Descend the staircase of locks, pass the pumping station at the Bottom Lock and join a grassy towpath. The M1 is on the left, while on the right is the London to Birmingham railway line. Pass beneath the dark railway bridge, then the A5 road bridge, and for the next 1¼ miles follow the canal through wide open countryside, enjoying the rural scenes.

3 At Norton Bridge cross the pretty wooden footbridge and follow the obvious path to the next bridge over the Grand

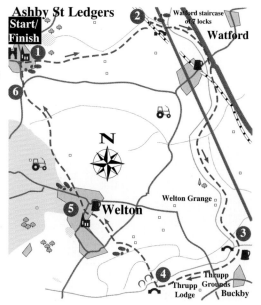

Union Canal. Rejoin the towpath and go right towards Braunston. Pass beneath Bridge No 8 at Thrupp Lodge and, in a further ½ mile, leave the canal at Bridge No 7 by joining the bridleway that crosses the bridge over the canal.

4 Pass through a gate, keeping a lookout for the bull. Locate a small wooden gate, with a hedge to your right. Continue ahead to cross a stream and bear left to a metal pole and stone stile, where an obvious field path leads to the road. Opposite is a public footpath sign to Welton and a field perimeter path takes you to the village.

5 Turn left and at the White Horse turn right along Well Lane to Ashby Road. Go left and in 100yds you reach a footpath sign on the right. Walk along the alleyway to a stone stile and cross the first field, heading slightly to the left. Although the footpath is not clear, a series of metal poles with white marker discs shows the way. At the brow of a hill follow a field path to the right to the next marker pole, where an obvious path leads you to Ashby St Ledgers.

6 When you reach the road, turn right and walk into the village, admiring the many thatched cottages on the way back to the church.

ALONG THE WAY

In a room above a timber-framed gatehouse in Ashby St Ledgers that still survives today, the conspirators of the Gunpowder Plot gathered. After the plot was discovered on 5 November 1605, Robert Catesby and his companions returned to the village from London, pausing briefly, before riding on to Holbeach. Three days later Catesby was shot and killed.

The locks at Watford descend 52ft 6in and an inclined plane similar to Foxton was envisaged but never implemented. At Watford Gap, four transport arteries are crammed into one corridor – M1, A5, Grand Union Canal and Birmingham to London Railway – and this makes an imposing sight from the towpath.

FACT FILE

Distance 7¼ miles
Time 2¾ hours
Maps OS Landranger 152, OS Pathfinder 977
Start Parish church of Blessed Virgin Mary and St Leodegarius, grid ref 574682
Terrain Good footpaths and canal towpath. No steep hills to climb
Nearest town Daventry
Parking Around church or in village
Refreshments The Stags Head, Watford; The White Horse, Welton
Public transport No service to Ashby St Ledgers, although walk could start at Welford.
Tel 01604 20077 for bus service details
Stiles Many stiles are enclosed with wire mesh and dogs will have to be lifted over
Suitable for Children and small dogs

The Stretton Hills of Salop

WEST MIDLANDS

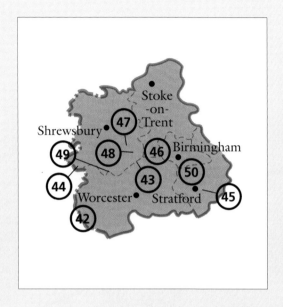

LORE AND LEGEND

A fishy tale and other stories add interest to a walk in peaceful, unspoilt countryside.

1 Cross the main road (notice the old milepost by the bus stop) and walk up the track beside the haulage yard, which bears the name A Howe. Turn right at two junctions. When you reach St Peter's Well Cottage notice the fish on the nameplate. The well itself is by the footpath. Keep going straight on.

2 Go through a gate and continue past a barn, keeping close to the field edge. The path climbs gently and you're channelled between two woods. Go through a gate in the corner between the woods and carry on uphill until a hunting gate gives access to Blakemere Hill Wood on your right.

3 Turn left as far as another gate. Don't go through it but turn right and follow the waymarks through a plantation. You now come to two adjacent junctions; turn right at the first, go straight on at the second, and maintain the same direction through all subsequent junctions and also after leaving the plantation. Pass a barn and a trig point at 831ft. The view includes the Black Mountains, Sugar Loaf, May Hill, Marcle Ridge and the Malverns.

4 Turn left at a lane, then take the first right. Turn right at the next junction and very soon you enter Birchypark Wood. Go straight on to a junction near a covered reservoir. Turn right then left through conifers to join a forest road. Forestry operations may obscure the route but it's difficult to go wrong. Follow the road to Poston Lodge Farm.

5 Left by a tennis court, through double gates and straight on, down steep-sided Cwm Du. Climb a stile into a cottage garden, pass through a former farmyard and turn left to another stile in a field corner. Walk ahead over two more fields, crossing a brook and climbing a slope to Vowchurch Common. Turn right and walk to main road. Cross and follow a lane through Vowchurch and Turnastone.

6 Join a bridleway on a bend next to an ochre-coloured house. Go straight on for 1 mile, then cross two footbridges and a stile. Go diagonally left across two fields, then turn right along a lane to find another footpath by the River Dore, then bears right to join the road near a brick cottage. Turn left, back into Peterchurch.

FACT FILE

Distance 7 miles
Time 3 hours
Maps OS Landranger 149 or 161, OS Pathfinder 1039
Start Peterchurch, grid ref 345385
Terrain Gentle; muddy in places
Nearest town Hay
Parking Peterchurch Picnic Place
Refreshments Boughton Arms and Post Office Stores, Peterchurch

Public transport Stagecoach Red & White 39 Hereford-Hay-Brecon Monday to Saturday; tel 01633 266336
Stiles Several; two awkward ones are easily avoided
Suitable for Children and dogs

ALONG THE WAY

The Golden Valley is green, not gold. The name comes from the river; to the original Welsh inhabitants it was simply dwr (water) but the Normans heard this as d'or (golden). So today we have the River Dore and the Golden Valley. Folklore has it that St Peter consecrated the well which bears his name and which is associated with various legends. Look inside St Peter's church to find out more.

WILD WYRE

Plantagenet kings used to hunt fallow deer in Wyre Forest. Today we can watch them instead, along with all the other wildlife which makes a woodland walk such a pleasure at any time of year.

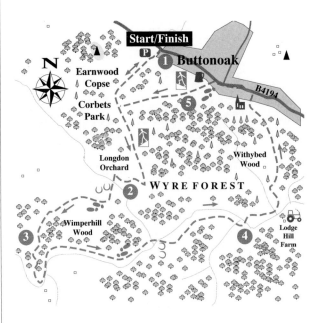

1 Follow a wide bridleway into the forest, ignoring all turnings. At a T-junction turn left on a forest road. This very soon crosses what looks like a firebreak but is actually the route of the Elan Valley pipeline, bringing Welsh water to Birmingham. Stay on the forest road and you'll eventually reach a crossroads where two signs read No Horses Please. Turn right here.

2 After a short distance turn left between two fenced areas, then at the next junction go straight on. After crossing a brook the path climbs to another crossroads. Turn right, passing through conifers, catching glimpses of fields through the trees on your right. Continue through an oakwood then through birches to the forest road, where you turn right.

FACT FILE

Distance 6 miles
Time 2½ hours
Maps OS Landranger 138, OS Pathfinder 67/77
Start/parking Small, unsigned Forestry Commission car park on south side of B4194 at Buttonoak, just to the west of Clematis Cottage, grid ref 747783
Terrain Gentle with excellent paths; one very small boggy section and one shallow stream to ford
Nearest town Bewdley
Refreshments The Button Oak near car park
Public transport Go Whittle bus 125 on Kidderminster–Bridgnorth route
Stiles Just 3, all at Buttonoak, 2 of them easily avoided
Suitable for Children, dogs on leads

3 After a few yards turn left on a grassy ride which twists and turns downhill – it eventually grows rather faint and boggy but then suddenly delivers you on to a wide bridleway by Dowles Brook, which forms the county boundary. Turn left, noticing the bat boxes fixed to the trees here. Keep the brook to your right, passing several footbridges and fords, until eventually you have no option but to cross over. Continue in the same direction, with the brook now on your left. After ½ mile you'll need to ford a shallow tributary and in a few more yards a footbridge allows you to cross back over Dowles Brook into Shropshire.

4 Keep going in the same direction, with Dowles Brook now on your right again. Very soon you pass Coopers Mill Youth Centre and shortly after this the path starts to climb and then forks. Keep left on the higher path which climbs gently out of the valley. Stay on the main path, ignoring any turnings. Eventually you reach a major junction which has rustic wooden signposts. Go straight on here and again at the next junction. Join the road next to a church and turn left.

5 Join a footpath next to the pub. After crossing a field bear right on the pipeline route seen earlier. When you reach the forest road make two right turns to return to car park or bus stop.

ALONG THE WAY

Wyre Forest straddles the Shropshire–Worcestershire border. It has excellent public access, yet remains relatively unknown, especially on the Shropshire side of Dowles Brook. It contains one of the largest areas of semi-natural ancient woodland in Britain, including old meadows and orchards. A large part is managed as a National Nature Reserve by English Nature. A hide is available for deer-watching (book at Callow Hill Visitor Centre, on A456 near Bewdley, tel 01299 266302) but you'll probably see deer anyway while walking in the forest. Squirrels are also common and there's a good range of birds, including dippers, grey wagtails and kingfishers along Dowles Brook.

WHERE BUZZARDS FLY

An exhilarating upland walk in which you're likely to have only sheep, rabbits, kestrels and buzzards for company. Choose a clear day to enjoy the magnificent views over England and Wales.

1 Join Offa's Dyke Path (ODP) behind the centre. After a few yards you enter England. Soon after that, having crossed the River Teme and the railway, you begin the long slog up Panpunton. Once on top the going is easy along the pronounced earthwork of Offa's Dyke. There are frequent signposts and waymarks.

2 When you reach the trig point on Cwm-sanaham Hill you're at 1,340ft. It's a good place for a break to watch the buzzards soaring over the Teme Valley far below. When you've finished, retrace your steps downhill for about 300yds to a bridleway which crosses the footpath. Leave ODP and turn left on the bridleway. From now on the paths are less clear and you need to pay close attention.

3 The bridleway passes a barn and goes along two field edges to reach an avenue of beech trees. Go through an old iron gate and turn right through the trees. At the far end of the avenue continue in the same direction to the left of the fence. At the bottom of the field climb over a fence and go straight on to the corner of the next field. Turn left, passing through an overgrown section, then hop over two strands of barbed wire and continue to the left of the hedge.

4 You should now be approaching New House Farm. The right of way is straight ahead through the farmyard but various obstacles make it necessary to skirt around the farm. Keep going until you find an easy place to climb the fence on your right, but look out for the hidden barbed wire. Carry on in the same direction, soon joining an obvious green lane which runs parallel with the farm drive.

5 You arrive at a junction known as Five Turnings. Join the track to Five Turnings Farm. This soon becomes a green lane then a field-edge path. Easy to follow, it goes straight ahead along the shoulder of Stow Hill (1,409ft). After 2 miles another path crosses it. Turn right, passing a pool then gradually bear right to meet a holloway (a sunken road, worn down from constant use) near Holloway Rocks. This descends steeply, soon becoming a major track which takes you down to Stowe church. Continue past the church to join a lane and keep going down.

6 You soon reach a junction where you turn right along a gated track. At a cattle grid turn left uphill, then cross another track at the top. Go through the left-hand gate to join a field-edge path which goes more or less straight ahead to the A488.

FACT FILE

Distance 10 miles
Time 4½ hours
Maps OS Landranger 137 or 148, OS Pathfinder 950
Start/parking Offa's Dyke Centre, West St, Knighton, grid ref 285725
Terrain Mostly undemanding but the initial climb is steep; many paths are neglected and lack waymarking
Nearest town Knighton
Refreshments Knighton
Public transport Trains on Heart of Wales line; Midland Red West buses from Ludlow, with direct connections to Shrewsbury, Hereford, Birmingham etc – tel 01345 212555
Stiles Many; also locked gates and fences to climb
Suitable for Anyone who can cope with stiles, gates and fences

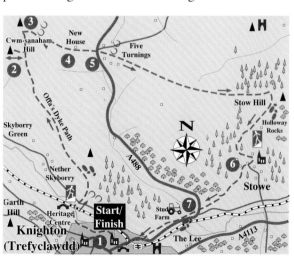

7 Cross the road to join another path – this then bears left to the point where the plantation ahead (Kinsley Wood) meets the road. You'll find a stile and some steps under a large sycamore tree. Go into the plantation and walk straight ahead, crossing the forest road, until you find a footpath that leads you through the trees. This path then emerges on the road opposite Knighton rail station. The town centre is a little further on.

ALONG THE WAY

Clun Forest is a region of hills, not trees as you might think. It is one of about a dozen ESAs – Environmentally Sensitive Areas – in which farmers are encouraged to preserve and enhance the traditional landscape.

The Heart of Wales line has survived 14 attempts at closure. The Ramblers' Association, Regional Railways and local councils are involved in various initiatives to promote its use by walkers. There are guided walks, free walks booklets for Rambler Ticket holders and circular tours using connecting buses.

THATCHES AND WELLS

Follow the field paths and bridleways that link two pretty Warwickshire villages,
each nestling in its own valley.

1 From Combrook's unusual church walk north along the signed no through road to reach a row of thatched cottages. Go left along the signed, enclosed bridleway and eventually enter woodland along the edge of a pool. Following a clear track, leave the trees to head across parkland, aiming just to the right of detached houses at Park Farm. When you reach the farm drive go right and follow it to the B4086.

2 Go left along the road and then turn right at the Lodge just before the crossroads. Walk across a cattle grid and follow the surfaced drive to make a right then a left turn, near farm buildings. Follow the clear, but now unsurfaced, track for another ¾ mile to a road. Cross here to follow the narrow, unfenced road opposite for ½ mile until you reach a T-junction. About 200yds before it a tarmac road goes right, towards Hillfields. To take the shorter route, turn right here and follow it for about 400yds to point 6, where you turn right again to rejoin the longer route.

3 At the T-junction go right and then left through the gateway and over the cattle grid for Westfields Stables. Follow the drive, which is initially surfaced, between the buildings eventually to meet a narrow lane. Turn right and follow the lane into Lighthorne.

4 Leaving Lighthorne retrace your steps along the narrow lane and immediately over the bridge go left on an enclosed path, through trees, to a hunter's gate. Entering rough pasture walk straight on along the right edge, soon bearing slightly left, to continue following the right boundary fence, still in the same field. This brings you to the top right corner –

cross a stile and go straight ahead across the narrow field. In a larger field follow the right hedge to a corner and pass through two gates, right of farm buildings, to reach a road.

5 Go left along the road for 50yds and turn right along the drive for Bannisters Meadow Farm. When you reach a junction in front of some farm buildings, go right through a gate which has some blue waymarks, and along the left edge of a large field. This takes you well right of Hillfields to reach its tarmac service road.

6 Go over the road and cross a large field, on a line for Compton Verney Hall, which you can see in the distance. You eventually reach a hedgerow – go through a gap, over a stream and into a narrow field. Carry on to the near corner – just before it go right again through a gap in the hedge and then turn left to reach the unfenced road. Cross two fields to reach a point near the left end of a line of tall redwood trees. Cross a fence to go diagonally left to enter trees. Go over a footbridge, onto the B4086 at the entrance to Compton Verney Hall.

7 Walk right along the road for a few yards and at some 'Reduce Speed Now' signs go left into a field. Aiming diagonally right, walk up to the rounded protruding corner of woodland. Entering this at a gatepost follow the obvious wide track straight ahead through the trees, all the way to a stile. It reduces to a very narrow path near the end. Cross into a sloping pasture and descend half-right to houses and a gate onto a road. Turn left for Combrook church.

FACT FILE

Distance 5 or 8 miles
Time 2½ or 4 hours
Maps OS Landranger 151, OS Pathfinder 998
Start Combrook church, grid ref 308517
Terrain Gently undulating, mainly bridleway and field paths. Can be muddy in Knightley's Coppice
Nearest town Stratford-upon-Avon

Parking Roadside in Combrook or Lighthorne – please consider local residents
Public transport None
Refreshments Bar meals at the Antelope pub, Lighthorne
Stiles Two, easy
Suitable for Children and dogs

ALONG THE WAY

Both Combrook and Lighthorne shelter in shallow valleys and contain a mix of old thatch and more recent architecture. The local stone resembles parts of the Cotswolds, while each village has its own elegant well. Both villages have many tiny footpaths to explore. Combrook church is built in a rococo style.

EDGE OF THE WILDERNESS

Enjoy high-level views on this classic walk that takes you to the
borders with Worcestershire and Shropshire.

1 From the bottom of Holy Austin Rock follow the stepped
path to the edge top. Go right to follow the main edge path
past a trig point until you arrive at the signpost denoting
the junction of three long distance routes. Go right
with the waymarked bridleway. When it swings sharp
left go right, through a vehicle barrier on a clear
path. At another barrier go left down the steps
and follow this path to a lane.

2 Turn right to follow the lane edge to reach
woodland and a public footpath sign on the left.
Go left and follow marker posts through the
trees to a kissing gate and into pasture. Turn
right to cross a stile in the corner and go through
a gate at Vale Head Farm. Bear left through the
farmyard to the front of a large barn. Go right
through a waymarked gap into another field. Cross to
a kissing gate and then over two stiles to meet a road
at some conifers.

3 Go left along the road and shortly right with the footpath sign
along the farm road for Lydiates Farm. In front of the farmhouse go right to a gate and kissing
gate. Clay pigeon shooting takes place here on Sunday mornings and Tuesday evenings. The
club operates a marshalling system whereby a steward stops the shooting and you are escorted
across the firing area. Through the gate follow the grassy track behind the farmhouse to reach
a stile into a large field. Cross this to the far left corner and a pylon, where you descend to
cross a stile into trees. Follow the path down and up the other side into a field. Go diagonally
right across it to the top right corner and a house. Cross a stile and follow the right edge of the
next field up to a minor road.

4 Turn right and follow the road to the entrance to Compton Park Farm. Turn right along
the drive and just before the house go right through a gate. Follow a tractor track through a
gate and right of barns to descend to the next corner where you pass through the right-hand of
two gates. Now with the left field boundary descend to a stile into The Wilderness. Head along
the clear path, down to a gate. Go through this and follow a green lane to cross two gated step
stiles. Follow the lane to a surfaced one. Go left for ¾ mile, to the T-junction at Herons Gate.

5 Turn right and follow the narrow lane up to the 'Staffordshire' sign. About 15yds after this
go through the gate on the left to follow a track until it becomes hedged on both sides. Go
right over a waymarked step stile into a field. Follow the right hedge/fence for this and two
more fields to go through double gates onto a hedged, unsurfaced farm road. Turn right and
follow the farm road through gates and past farm buildings to a T-junction with a narrow
surfaced road.

6 Turn left along the road for about 70yds and then go right with a footpath sign over a gated
step stile. Take the track across the field and when you meet a hedge bear right to follow it to a
corner. Entering another field follow the hedge to a corner, a pool and a gate. Staying in the
field go right to follow the hedgerow to the next corner where there is another pool. Go right
for about 40yds to a stile on the left. Cross it and walk through the few trees to the marker
post in front.

7 You are now on the edge of The Sheepwalks. Follow the marker posts over the steep hill and down the other side to a gated step stile. Climb this to rejoin the left woodland fence and follow it to its pointed end. Leave the fence to walk forward along the higher point and descend to a gate and step stile. On the other side a clear track takes you down to pass through a gate and arrive at the right corner of a pool. Next to the fence there is a waymarked gated step stile. Cross this and another stile to pass between the brick barn and the pool; you soon arrive at a stile and hunter's gate (narrow gate for horses). Cross into the parkland pasture and walk across to the step stile opposite and next to Enville Hall.

8 At the ornamental gates go right and then right again through white wooden gate posts to join the Staffordshire Way. Now follow the narrow fenced road to pass a pool. As the road swings right continue along a sunken unsurfaced lane. Stay with this and in about ½ mile cross a tarmac road into another sunken unsurfaced lane. Follow this down and then up to meet another road on a corner. Go right for 100yds and opposite a road junction turn left with the Staffordshire Way sign. Walk on a clear path first through trees then past houses, to follow a fence and a field edge; you eventually arrive at a field crossing before houses. Cross to the houses and follow the enclosed path between them to a road. Turn right to a T-junction and go right again. Just past the last house go right into the trees along a path and in a little while left up to the road at your start point.

The stunning view from the Sheepwalks towards the Clent hills

ON BENTHALL EDGE

The Unesco World Heritage Site at Ironbridge is famous for its industrial history but it's the lovely countryside of Benthall Edge that is the focus for this walk.

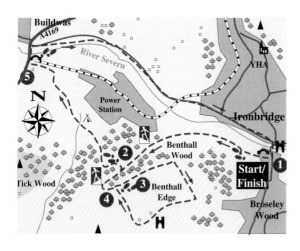

1 Having explored Ironbridge, cross the bridge itself and turn right into Benthall Edge Wood. It doesn't matter which path you choose initially as long as you end up following the dismantled railway line along the northern edge of the wood – you can't miss it. On the far side join a path leading uphill in the shadow of the power station. At a junction turn right on the lower of two paths.

2 Soon after you pass an area of grassland another path appears, more or less parallel, but lower. The two begin to converge and when they meet you turn a sharp corner to walk just inside the southern edge of the wood. You soon come to a stile, where you briefly leave the wood for a few yards before turning sharp left to re-enter it. Continue along the inside edge to a cottage.

3 Bear left and go deeper into the wood. The path meanders to a T-junction where you turn right to leave the wood on a tree-lined green lane. When this bends left go through a kissing gate on the right and straight ahead to Benthall Hall. Pass the Hall and church and cross an avenue to a green lane. Turn right to return to Benthall Edge Wood, entering it by the stile that you encountered earlier.

4 Turn left, returning to the sharp corner where two major paths meet. Take the lower one this time. It soon leaves the wood and heads downhill as a surfaced track. When it bends left go straight on instead, walking towards The Wrekin. Pass to the left of a pylon and keep more or less straight on through Pool View Caravan Park. Follow the access road all the way to the A4169 and don't be tempted to follow any of the waymarkers that you encounter on the way, as the footpaths are obstructed.

5 When you reach the road you'll see the entrance to Buildwas Abbey signed on the left. Turn right to cross the Severn, then right again towards Ironbridge. Very soon a stile gives access to the riverbank and you can follow the Severn all the way back to the iron bridge itself.

FACT FILE

Distance 6 miles
Time 2½ hours
Maps OS Landranger 127, OS Pathfinder 890
Start The Iron Bridge at Ironbridge Gorge, grid ref 672034
Terrain Gentle; some mud and long grass
Nearest town Telford
Parking There are several car parks in Ironbridge, on both sides of the river
Refreshments Ironbridge
Public transport Frequent daily buses from most parts of Shropshire, also from Stafford, Wolverhampton and Birmingham; many buses connect with trains at Wellington and Telford; contact Traveline on 01345 056785
Stiles Only a couple
Suitable for Children and dogs

ALONG THE WAY

It was at Ironbridge and neighbouring Coalbrookdale that Abraham Darby I changed the world in the early 18th century when he transformed the production of cast iron, making possible the Industrial Revolution. His grandson Abraham Darby III was responsible for building the world's first iron bridge here in 1779. Today the industrial sites and museums offer something of interest for everyone.

Benthall Hall is a fine 16th century stone house. The Benthalls still live there but sadly they're just tenants now – the house belongs to the National Trust and it's open to the public on Wednesday, Sunday and Bank Holiday afternoons in summer.

WOODLAND TREK

Woods and water combine to give a walk which is beautiful at any time,
and which provides shelter from the elements in winter.

1 Walk up Station Road in the direction of Highley. When you reach the main road turn left,
then right down Netherton Lane. Soon after passing Whitehouse Farm turn onto an unsigned
footpath on the left. This starts off as a farm lane then continues along field edges. It then goes
down the middle of more fields to reach the B4555 close to a farm. Turn right. There are
some nasty bends on this road and if you have young children with you it may be better to
miss this section out – to do this, simply follow Netherton Lane down to Borlemill instead of
joining the footpath near Whitehouse Farm.

2 After just under ½ mile join an easily missed footpath on the right and walk through
woodland to Netherton Lane at Borlemill. The footpath continues opposite, winding through
woods and meadows just to the east of Borle Brook. When you come to an old stone bridge
cross the brook to find three paths. Follow the middle one to a T-junction next to an iron
bridge which once carried a railway. Turn left, following a well-defined path which runs beside
a brook. The path, which is part of the Jack Mytton Way, is a permissive one and was once a
railway linking collieries with the Severn Valley Railway.

3 When you reach a lane turn right and cross over to join a bridleway. Follow a brook through
woodland to a clearing and turn right. Go through birch woodland to emerge into a field.
Keep more or less straight on, passing to the left of a house. The route is now waymarked,
guiding you round the house to join the driveway. When this bends to the left keep walking
straight on across fields to reach a lane opposite the pub at Billingsley.

4 Turn right, then left towards New England and Highley. This ridge-top lane gives good
views before descending to Borle Brook. As you approach a ford join a footpath on the right
which goes to the iron railway bridge that you saw earlier in the walk. Turn left to recross the
stone bridge and bear left uphill to a lane. Turn right, then join the first footpath on the right.
Bear left across a large field to a hedge-corner, go through a gap and walk along a field edge.
Cross part of a golf course, turn left through trees, then follow signs across the rest of the golf
course to a lane.

5 Turn left, then quite soon go right towards the centre of Highley. Opposite the youth club
turn left down a no through road. After about 300yds fork right to descend through woods to
the country park. Cross the railway and turn right. Near the Ship Inn is a path which leads to
Highley station. The car park is just a little further up the lane.

FACT FILE

Distance 8 miles
Time 3 hours
Maps OS Landranger 138,
OS Pathfinder 932
Start/parking Severn Valley
Country Park, Station Road,
Highley, grid ref 746830
Terrain Gentle but muddy
Nearest town Bridgnorth
Refreshments The Cape of
Good Hope at Billingsley,
Ship Inn near Highley
Station, shops in Highley
village, station buffet when
trains are running
Public transport Buses on
Kidderminster–Bridgnorth
routes; Whittles 125 calls at
Highley while Midland Red
West 297 calls at Alveley (over
the river – cross footbridge in
country park); trains on
Severn Valley Railway to
Highley Station
Stiles A few
Suitable for Children and
dogs – one bit of road
unsuitable for young children
can be avoided

ALONG THE WAY

It's hard to believe that this
was once a quarrying and
coalmining area. Quarrying
has a long history – some of
the stone for Worcester
Cathedral came from Highley
and was sent downstream by
boat. Coalmining began in the
Middle Ages but was small-
scale until the 19th century.
The last colliery closed in
1969 and since then the old
industrial sites have been
transformed into a country
park which straddles the
Severn – make sure you head
for the west bank for this
walk. Anybody with an
interest in industrial
archaeology will enjoy
searching for traces of the old
mineral railways in the lovely
woods around Borle Brook
and its tributaries.

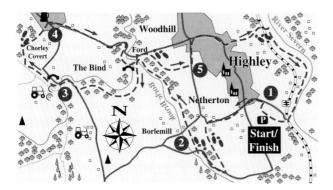

LAND OF THE MARCHER LORD

Mortimer Forest provides endless opportunities for fine walks with magnificent views – this one, just outside Ludlow, is one of the best.

1 Turn left in front of Ludlow Castle and walk along Dinham, continuing downhill to cross the River Teme at Dinham Bridge. Follow the lane to the right, going straight on at a junction along a no through road. You'll see a stile on the left – you have a choice of road or footpath, but if you choose the footpath you'll soon have to return to the road. At Priors Halton the no through road becomes a bridleway and enters Oakly Park.

2 Join a bridleway on the left and follow it for 2 miles. Another bridleway is signed at Lady Halton Farm – don't join it, and don't turn left into the farmyard. Soon after passing Poles Farm you reach a lane.

3 Turn right and enter the Forestry Commission's Deep Wood. Continue to a junction where a left turn takes you uphill on the main forest road. Cross the Elan Valley pipeline (bringing Welsh water to Birmingham) and keep going uphill to a junction where you turn left to reach a pumping station. Continue along the waymarked path.

4 When you see a small gate on the left, turn right uphill. Cross a forest road and continue to a public one. Turn right for 60yds then cross to a footpath. Walk over a field, then turn left to pass behind a barn and go straight ahead on an obvious path. Ignore all turnings.

5 At a nine-ways junction continue on the same path. It's easy to distinguish – it's a sunken track, while the others are modern forest paths. Before long you'll be walking along the edge of the forest and pass through a deer gate. Keep going until you come to a road.

6 Turn right to Whitcliffe Common. There are so many paths here that specific directions are worthless. Basically, a left turn takes you back to Dinham Bridge; while a right turn takes you down to Ludford Bridge. You can return to Ludlow either way, and the two bridges are connected by a riverside path, in addition to the many paths that lead through the trees.

ALONG THE WAY

There are wonderful views throughout this walk, but especially from the path along the edge of the forest. You can see the full 16 mile length of Wenlock Edge, as well as Long Mynd, the Strettons, the Clees, and the Wrekin. There are also good views of Ludlow, and of Downton Castle in Herefordshire, a pseudo-medieval fortress built in 1778 for a Ludlow MP.

Mortimer Forest includes former Saxon hunting forest given by William I to Ralph Mortimer after the Conquest. Created Earl of March, Mortimer and his descendants virtually ruled the border country for the next 300 years from their castles at Wigmore and Ludlow.

FACT FILE

Distance 8 miles
Time 3 hours
Maps OS Landranger 137 or 138, OS Pathfinder 951
Start Castle Square, Ludlow, grid ref 509746
Terrain Easy, with two very slight climbs; muddy in places
Nearest town Ludlow
Parking Car parks off Castle Square or Galdeford, Ludlow
Refreshments Ludlow; try the historic Feathers Hotel

Public transport Daily trains on Cardiff-Manchester line; frequent Monday to Saturday buses operated mainly by Midland Red West from Shrewsbury, Hereford, Kidderminster, Birmingham and Welsh border towns; sparse Sunday buses from Hereford, Kidderminster and Birmingham operated by West Midlands Travel and Go Whittle; details from Shropshire Traveline on 01345 056785
Stiles A few, all avoidable
Suitable for Children and dogs

There are excellent views of Ludlow and the Clee hills near the end of the walk

SHAKESPEARE COUNTRY

Take a walk with literary connections along one of the most scenic canals in the country.

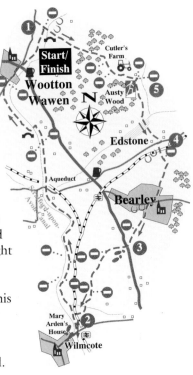

1 At the pull-in, follow the waymarked bridleway south-east to meet the Stratford-upon-Avon canal. Walk south along the towpath for 4 miles until you reach Wilmcote moorings and a road bridge. Leave the towpath here and cross the bridge into Wilmcote.

2 From Wilmcote retrace your steps to the canal and follow the towpath north to a point, just past the end of the moorings, where there is a small, weighted metal gate on the right. Go through this and follow the enclosed path over a drive and across the railway line into a field. Follow the left hedge for half its length to go left into another field. Here go diagonally right (35°) to a gap in a stranded hedge. Now in a huge field go forward (a 20° direct bearing) to eventually meet a line of four oak trees. Walk to the oak on the right end and continue forward (85°) across the field to meet the A34.

3 Go left for 30yds and then head right along an enclosed bridleway. Merging with a roughly surfaced lane, continue ahead into Bearley. Turn right and, just past the church, go left at the letterbox to follow School Lane down to pass Grange Road. Here continue ahead along a clear bridleway to eventually go over the Edstone Hall level crossing and then straight on to the road.

4 Turn right along the road for 75yds and then left along the surfaced bridleway. Follow this through the parkland of the Edstone Estate for ¾ mile until you arrive at Cutler's Farm.

5 Immediately past the farmhouse go left through the waymarked gate and the former farmyard. Now carry on straight ahead up the edge of two fields to arrive at some woodland. Here go right to a hunter's gate into the trees and then follow a clear bridleway all the way back to the canal. Cross the bridge and retrace your steps to the pull-in.

The Stratford-upon-Avon canal at Wooton Wawen

ALONG THE WAY

The Stratford-upon-Avon canal is noted as one of the most scenic in the country and along the length covered by this walk you cross two remarkable cast-iron aqueducts. Wilmcote is a small, attractive village that is famous for Mary Arden's House. This childhood home of Shakespeare's mother is open to the public and is very close to the canal.

FACT FILE

Distance 10 miles
Time 5 hours
Maps OS Landranger 151, OS Pathfinder 975 & 997
Start Pull-in on Pettiford Lane, Wootton Wawen, grid ref 161638
Terrain Easy walking. There is a section of field crossings where compass bearings are given to aid navigation. During winter it can be muddy in Austy Wood. Walk crosses two railway lines that are in use. Take great care!
Nearest town Stratford-upon-Avon

Parking At the start or Bearley Aqueduct, grid ref 162609
Public transport You can take a British Rail train to Wilmcote and join the walk there
Refreshments Pubs in Wilmcote
Stiles Four
Suitable for Older children. Dogs under close control

EAST ANGLIA

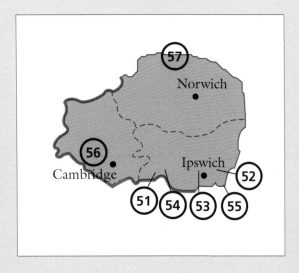

CAMPING GROUND

This isolated corner of Cambridgeshire has numerous footpaths on the county's highest ground. Walk through its charming camp settlements, including the original Castle Camps site at the church and moat.

1 Set off eastwards on the lane signed to Haverhill, with its large houses and chestnut trees. Take the signed footpath between boarded fences to the right. Cross the stile before the handgate and continue on the boundary to a ditch. Go left, over three stiles, right over a bridge, then left on the field edge. At the end of the hedge turn 60° right across a field to a bridleway.

2 Follow the bridleway left between hedges – it curves right to reach a lane. Go right, through the village to a T-junction and 1993 Parish Council centenary village sign and seat.

3 Turn left and immediately right, taking the second of two tracks at Rose Cottage. An excellent green path goes over the field. At the T-junction go right to the bushes and then curve left to the church by way of a seat and kissing gates. Between the kissing gates, on the right, the uneven ground was once the site of the village; the castle moat was on the left.

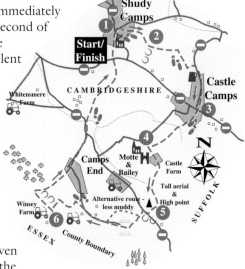

4 Ignore the signs and stiles and keep to the farm road until it turns into the yard. Don't enter but go straight ahead over a fence and on to a track, then arc right to the remains of the perimeter track. Follow it right on the farmer's preferred route to pass the tall mast. Turn off right, crossing to the left of the trees, then round the dyke to the lane and footpath sign.

5 Take the bridleway left beside the mast (usually muddy at the start). Now either follow it to the lane or just beyond the compound, cross a grill bridge. Head for the left corner of the trees, then go left on a path to the lane. Continue north-west to a corner, then turn off left down Winsey Farm access road. About 300yds short of the farm turn right with a hedge and ditch on the right – here you are on the county boundary with Suffolk.

6 Go through the hedge and turn right, then go straight ahead to emerge at Camps End. Turn left on a lane. At the T- junction go left down the dip to a footpath sign on the right. Cross the stile, walk up the field edge, cross another stile and continue onto a farm track. At the end cross the field, heading right to the left end of the copse where you cross a footbridge. Go right and left, heading towards the church and then a lane. Cross another footbridge and field; just before the road enter the bushes on the left. Cross a stile to the grass field, emerging near the church.

Looking down the valley approaching Shudy Camps

ALONG THE WAY

Castle Camps was deserted in the 17th century when its residents left to avoid the plague. It all became very lively again with the building of the 1940/46 airfield, which was the first to operate Mosquitoes. A memorial to units based here was dedicated in September 1994 at grid ref 637429. Evidence at Shudy shows that it was once an extensive Roman and Anglo-Saxon area.

FACT FILE

Distance 6 miles
Time 3½ hours
Maps OS Landranger 154, OS Pathfinder 1028
Start/parking On verge opposite Shudy church, grid ref 620444
Terrain Gentle slopes, some arable fields and chance of mud
Nearest town Haverhill in Suffolk
Refreshments Two pubs at Castle Camps
Public transport Cambus 136 Haverhill–Cambridge, tel 01223 423554 and Heddingham Buses, Haverhill–Audley End
Stiles Several, with high steps
Suitable for Older children and dogs

BURIED TREASURE

This walk features the River Deben and a visit to the site of the
famous Anglo-Saxon ship burial at Sutton Hoo.

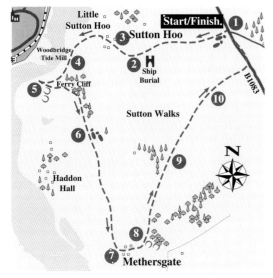

1 Cross the road and take the sandy track
signposted public Footpath to River Deben.

2 The barrows of the ship burial are small
grassy humps fenced off on your left, unim-
pressive perhaps until you remember that they
have been there for 1,500 years. Bear right on
a track descending towards the river. When
you come into an open field, bear right
through woods to Little Sutton Hoo.

3 Turn left, where there is a signpost, on a
track which soon becomes a clear path. Keep
straight on past a wooden generator hut and
cross a reed-choked stream on a footbridge to
reach the river.

4 Follow the path through woods along the
shore, with views of Woodbridge.

5 When you are directly opposite the Tide Mill, a white wooden building, the path climbs
steeply left up Ferry Cliff. At the top, turn left and follow the edge of the wood (signposted).

6 At the corner of the wood (no signpost), strike right across a well-trodden path to a gap in
the hedge. Follow the track straight ahead to Methersgate Hall.

7 Go round the buildings, following a sign to Apple House, then through a gate in the white
paling fence on your left to a track between houses.

8 The official route goes left after the last cottage; take care as the bridleway is sometimes
badly obstructed. At the end of the first field, go slightly left to a gap in the hedge, then keep
to the right-hand edge of the next field and follow the track through a wood.

9 At the fence, turn right, then left at the signpost on a grass track. At a field corner, go
straight on across a cultivated field, aiming for the isolated tree in the far hedge. Cross the next

field, aiming to strike the
next boundary at the low
point of the slight dip, and
then hold the same line
across the corner of the next
field. Aim towards a wide gap
in the conifer belt fringing
the track on your left, well to
the right of the tall Scots
pines.

10 Turn right up the track,
then left on the B road to the
start.

*This walk takes you through pleasant
woodland*

FACT FILE

Distance 7 miles
Time 3 hours
Map OS Landranger 169
Start/parking Junction of
B1083 Bawdsey road with
minor road to Hollesley, grid
ref 298491
Terrain - Mainly easy; can be
muddy and overgrown in
woods; two cultivated fields
near end
Nearest town Woodbridge
Refreshments None on route
Public transport Information
from County Connections, tel
01473 265676
Stiles None
Suitable for Children

ALONG THE WAY

Sutton Hoo consists of a
dozen burial mounds or
barrows. One was excavated
in 1939. It contained the
remains of a wooden ship,
filled with the possessions of
a king. These included
weapons, a stone sceptre
surmounted by a stag and
jewellery, including an
intricate gold buckle and an
enamelled purse-lid.

WINDING WATERWAYS

This linear walk follows the course of a canal which was once the lifeblood of industry in this area.

1 From Ipswich station, turn right and follow the road, then go left at The Defiance pub to Stoke Bridge and Ipswich Wet Dock.

2 Cross Stoke Bridge and descend to the start of the towpath. At Constantine Weir, the river ceases to be tidal.

3 Go left on Paper Mill Lane to a footbridge over the river, and continue on the west bank through meadows. This section can flood in winter; if it does you follow Paper Mill Lane to Claydon.

4 At Great Blakenham, cross the river at a bridge over a disused lock. Pass the houses called Bridgewaters and Mill Cottage and, just in front of Herb Cottage, turn right down a passageway back to the river, now a narrow, reedy stream.

5 As you reach Causeway Lake, the stream suddenly widens again into a broad, stately river lined with weeping willows and bulrushes.

6 At Baylham Mill, turn left up the lane, then right just before the railway level crossing. Follow the railway for a short distance until you meet the river again.

7 At the imposing Bosmere Mill, you can shorten the walk by following the road left to Needham Market railway station and getting a train back to the start.

8 There is a second chance to shorten the walk, at the substantial red-brick Hawks Mill, or you can divert to Fen Alder Carr Farm Tearooms for refreshments. The next 2 miles take you through willow meads and pastures.

9 Industry reappears as you enter Stowmarket. Cross the drive for Munton and Fison's factory and follow the river along their well-kept lawn. At the end of the factory, keep well to the left to pass the two settling tanks. Keep on along the river, past ICI's paint factory, crossing the two entrance driveways. At the end of the ICI factory, keep straight on along the river path until you come up some stone steps onto the Pickerel Bridge in the centre of Stowmarket. The railway station is just to your right. It will have taken you all day to walk here, and if you had made the journey by barge in the heyday of the Gipping Valley Navigation you would not have been much quicker. British Rail will return you to Ipswich in 12 minutes.

ALONG THE WAY

In 1790, the Ipswich and Stowmarket Navigation was completed, converting the meandering River Gipping into a reliable canal. Then, less than a century later, came the railway, and the canal fell swiftly into disuse. Suffolk County Council has now restored the entire towpath, from Stoke Bridge at Ipswich Port to Pickerel Bridge in Stowmarket, making a superb linear walk of 17 miles. Ipswich Wet Dock was constructed in the last century to give the port a reliable, non-tidal dock. It is still the base for modern shipping companies, and for Cranfields Flour and Pauls Malt. The attractive disused water mills at Sproughton, Baylham and Needham Market remind you that the river was earning its living as a power source long before the Navigation was built.

FACT FILE

Distance 12 or 17 miles
Time 5½ or 8 hours
Maps OS Landrangers 169 and 155
Start/parking Ipswich railway station, grid ref 157438. Fee £1 all day Saturdays, Sundays and Bank Holidays
Terrain Easy, well-maintained towpath
Nearest towns Ipswich and Stowmarket
Refreshments Ipswich, Needham Market and Stowmarket, pubs in Sproughton and Bramford
Public transport British Rail InterCity services at Ipswich and Stowmarket, more than once per hour; local British Rail service at Needham Market
Stiles Lots, all well-constructed and with space for dogs to get round or under
Suitable for Older children, energetic dogs

At Bosmere Mill you can shorten the walk

PICTURE POSTCARDS

Explore two Suffolk villages, right on the border with Essex, which have castle ruins, restored railway buildings, the Sue Ryder Museum and a vineyard.

1 From the picture-book village green in Cavendish walk a few yards into the village. On the left is The Bull pub which offers a range of Adnams Ales and boasts an Egon Ronay recommendation for its food. Opposite, a path leads along a gravel drive, through the grounds of the Sue Ryder Home. Bear left with the drive, then right towards a bridge across the stream but don't cross this – instead, keep to the left of the bank, continuing next to a fence. Cross a bridge and stile and follow until you reach the road.

2 Turn right into Pentlow Road, the site of the former Stour Valley railway station, closed in 1964. Cross the bridge over the railway and walk down the road into Essex. Stop to look at the circular tower of Pentlow church on the left before turning right into a signed bridleway by the fork in the road. After a few yards, cross to the other side of the ditch and follow the track. The path eventually dips down through some trees, then skirts the edge of a field. Pass Bower Hall, keeping straight ahead and continuing along a road. When the road bends to the left, take the track leading off to the right, marked by a blue arrow. Don't cross the river, but follow this track for quite a distance through open fields, enjoying the views across the Stour Valley. Eventually, turn sharp right

downhill, then go left along a road. At the end, bear right into a lane then, after a few yards, turn left into a path leading towards the river.

3 Cross the bridge and walk across the meadow, which you leave via a kissing gate by the old mill. Walk up the road to cross the former railway bridge. Turn left into Bailey Lane and continue along the path that leads off to the left into Clare Country Park. Walk along the former railway trackbed, crossing the river, and pass the priory on the left before you reach a road. Turn right and walk down to the main A1092 road. Turn right to walk past the many interesting buildings into the centre of Clare.

4 From The Bell hotel, turn right, passing the church of St Peter and St Paul. Bear left then right with the road, continuing along Bridewell Street before turning right into Hermitage Meadows, a new development. Go straight ahead along the track leading to Hermitage Farm and bear right here, following the yellow arrows. Go through a gap in the hedge and turn left to walk uphill. Enjoy the view as you look back towards Clare and follow the path which takes you through a line of trees, bearing left along the edge of a field. Turn sharp right to reach a high point before dipping down. Continue straight ahead at the diesel tank, passing a farmyard on the right, and follow the track downhill, turning right at the bottom. After a few yards, turn left across a bridge and stile, cross a bridged ditch and carry on uphill. When you reach a lane, turn right.

5 Go down the lane and follow it to the end, turning right by the entrance to the local vineyard. Walk back to the green at Cavendish, passing St Mary's church on the way, and allow time to explore this very pretty village.

FACT FILE

Distance 7½ miles
Time 3½ hours
Map OS Landranger 155
Start/parking Off the green at Cavendish
Terrain Easy going
Nearest towns Haverhill and Sudbury
Refreshments The Bull at Cavendish and The Bell at Clare are recommended, plus other pubs in both places
Public transport Beestons Coaches runs a regular Monday to Saturday service between Haverhill and Sudbury
Stiles Three easy ones
Suitable for Dogs on leads and children

ALONG THE WAY

The pretty village of Cavendish is on the River Stour and the church and village green have been featured on many calendars At the Sue Ryder Foundation a museum, which is open every day, details the work carried out there. Clare is believed to date back to the Iron Age and the castle originates from Norman times. The priory was built in the 13th century and there are many Tudor and medieval buildings in the town centre.

SHIPS AND SWANS

The Shotley peninsula lies between the two great estuaries of the Orwell and Stour. This route goes around the tip of Shotley Peninsula, returning past the lovely Tudor mansion of Erwarton Hall.

1 At the telephone box, turn right up the lane – this is tarmac at first, then it becomes a grass track between fields. At the end, turn left down the lane past Charity Farm.

2 At a row of brick cottages, turn right and follow a footpath sign up a sandy track, which swings left by a pair of brick semi-detached cottages to the river dyke.

3 Follow the path on top of the dyke eastward – the view on your left stretches across the river to Levington, with its hilltop church and yacht marina.

4 At the start of the hedge, follow the fore-shore until you reach a signpost. Climb back onto the dyke (now a well-trodden path all year round), and follow it for 1½ miles along the Lower Reach of the Orwell, usually crowded with yachts and commercial shipping. In places, the foreshore is a pleasantly sandy beach, and the drainage channel on the inland side of the dyke is home to ducks, moorhens and swans.

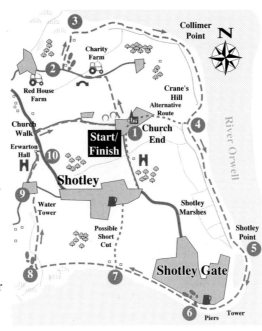

5 Follow the dyke left around Shotley Point Marina, then take the riverside road.

6 After the Bristol Arms pub, continue ahead on a path along the Stour, with a stile over a pipe crossing the path. Where dead trees block the foreshore, go right up some steps in the cliff. Turn left on a well-walked path, through woods, across the end of Stourside Street, and then follow waymarks to a path along the field edges above the river, with excellent views.

7 Cross the cinder track at a signpost and go past the front of Rose Farm Cottages, continuing along the field path (the track is a short cut back if necessary). As the marshes of Erwarton Bay appear below you, look out for a path left to the river dyke.

8 Cross a culvert – this is why you must be on the dyke – and turn right on a grassy track when you reach a signpost. At a rusty gate and pond, bear right, follow the track out to the road and turn left.

9 At Erwarton Hall, turn right up the lane, which is lined with the remains of ancient oak trees.

10 Turn left, then right up Church Walk to return to the start.

FACT FILE

Distance 8 miles (can be shortened)
Time- 3–4 hours
Map OS Landranger 169
Start/parking Shotley church, grid ref 236360 (for about eight cars – please give priority to churchgoers). Alternative start and parking at Shotley Gate
Terrain Mainly easy. Dyke overgrown in places in summer
Nearest town Ipswich
Refreshments Bristol Arms, Shotley Gate
Public transport County Connections, tel 01473 265676.
Stiles One, no problem for dogs
Not suitable for Small children. Those with hayfever should avoid the dyke at point 3 between May and September as it gets overgrown with grass. Take the track past the car park at the start to join the walk at point 4.

ALONG THE WAY

There is always shipping to watch at Harwich and Felixstowe. The estuaries are good for birdwatching, especially at low tide, and by October the first of the winter migrants should be arriving. The present Erwarton Hall (rebuilt 1575) is a fine red-brick Elizabethan mansion, and Anne Boleyn stayed at the earlier Erwarton Hall (owned by her uncle, Sir Philip Calthorpe), before her ill-starred marriage to Henry VIII.

DOWN BY THE RIVERSIDE

This walk from a key Roman river and road crossing town with its attractive waterside, takes you out and up into quiet countryside, then back via a marina complex and riverside path.

1 Head south past the water inlet and the B1043 road, turning right down Silver Street past several thatched cottages and out into a country lane which eventually becomes a track. Leave this where it goes left to Debden Top Farm, keeping straight ahead on a grassy track. At about 150ft, there are good views from here.

2 Go past a water tower, and at the end of the hedge at some trees turn right on a bridleway. Follow it past two woods on the left, then along a field edge to a farm road. Go left, then head for the main road.

3 Cross the road and go through a kissing gate. Bear slightly left to cross the railway at the white fence and warning lights. Go straight ahead over another stile and a weir, staying beside the thick hedge. This less distinct path bears right to emerge by a lock and the dangerously narrow Buckden Road. Go left over two bridges where the Ouse Way emerges on the left. Just past the Buckden Marina entrance follow the Ouse Way signs to the right.

4 Go straight ahead with a water ski lake on the left, keeping on the marina road past the holiday cabins. At the river follow the signed path over various stiles to reach a track to Buckden. There can be cattle along here and the path is very near the water.

5 Continue past a golf course into willow trees and then onto a concrete track. Follow this, bearing right to a T-junction. You can go right to Brampton Mill pub or continue left past boat moorings to reach a track signed Huntingdon and Godmanchester. Pass the barrier and continue on the tarmacked track – this takes you under two railway bridges to Port Holme meadows, once a racecourse and airfield.

6 Take the path ahead, aiming slightly to the right of Godmanchester church. Eventually you will see a notice and gate – go over the bridge with a lock on the right and then turn left to reach the Chinese Bridge and car parks.

FACT FILE

Distance 9 miles
Time 4½ hours
Maps OS Landranger 153, OS Pathfinders 960 and 981
Start/parking Chinese Bridge, Godmanchester, grid ref 224706 (another free car park 300yds north)
Terrain Easy, but riverside and water meadows impassable during flooding and can be muddy
Nearest town Huntingdon
Refreshments The Swan, Offord Cluny, The Horseshoe, Offord D'Arcy, and several places at the start
Public transport Godmanchester lies on various bus routes
Stiles Some narrow crush type and high steppers
Suitable for Not for disabled or buggies. Children should be closely supervised by water and railway crossing. Dogs should be kept on leads

ALONG THE WAY

Godmanchester was a Roman town and is encircled by ancient roads. The various bridges over the river, and the wealth of half-timbered and thatched cottages are so delightful, especially on a warm summer's day, that you may find yourself lingering too long to finish the walk.

Start the walk at the pretty Chinese Bridge at Godmanchester

HOLDING THE FORT

Circle inland from a 700-year-old port to welcoming villages, visiting an impressive Iron Age fort, and return beside salt marshes. A narrow gauge steam railway provides an interesting diversion.

1 Head south, passing the Catholic church and green, past the no through road sign, then bear right and left to the A149. Cross the road, going left and right, and continue down Market Lane to walk past the school. At the cemetery follow the track on the left, heading up past a farm to Gallow Hill. The top of Holkham church and monument can be seen over the trees on the right.

2 For the shorter walk take the first track on the left before the house and descend to cross the narrow gauge railway to reach the B1105. Turn left then right into Warham, passing the church to the welcoming pub, where you rejoin the longer route. Or, pass the house and take the track on the left for 1½ miles. Cross the railway to reach the B1105 at Wighton.

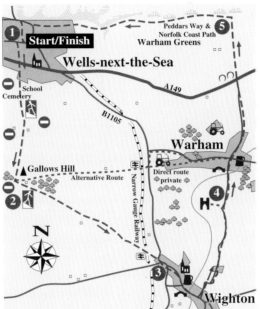

3 Walk ahead on the main road for 150yds, continuing through the village on the Binham/Holt road past the church and roadside seat. Pass the pub and cross the river to take the first turning on the left – this is Warham Road, a narrow byway with ivy-clad hedges. After about 1 mile turn off left on a track signed as a footpath to Camp Hills. Pause here to take a look at the impressive banks and ditches of an Iron Age fort beside the River Stiffkey.

4 Return to the lane and continue to Warham. All Saints church is on the left and the pub is at the crossroads. Carry on straight ahead past the parish garden and seat to the A149 coast road, crossing to a track leading to a gate and the Norfolk coast path beside the saltmarshes. Some of the buildings over to the right are remains of a wartime artillery range.

ALONG THE WAY

Wells harbour is not as busy with commercial traffic now, due to its difficult channel. However, a sail training ship from Holland and fishing boats are regular visitors.

The 10¼ inch narrow gauge steam railway that you pass at point 2 is the longest of its size in the world – its unique Garratt locomotive is necessary to climb the gradient. A timetable for the railway is available from the tourist information centre in Wells.

5 Follow the grassy path to the left – very high tides reach here and they leave a ribbon of debris, mainly of dead vegetation from the marsh. Skirt round to the left of a marshy inlet with its memorial seat, perhaps pausing to watch the flocks of birds and listen to the calls of the oyster catchers and curlews. Approaching Wells, loop round left into the bushes, then up onto a bank, built after the 1953 floods. Keep on the top to reach a group of old fishermen's sheds, now used for other trades. The road leads onto the main quay, past the grain elevator. Go right, following the tourist information centre sign to return to The Buttlands.

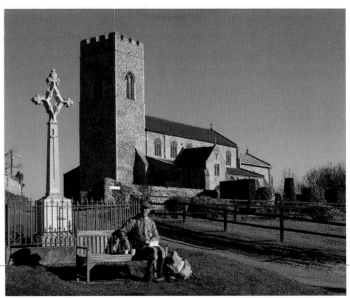

The seat at Wighton church is an ideal lunch spot

Snowdon from Penrhyndeudraeth

WALES

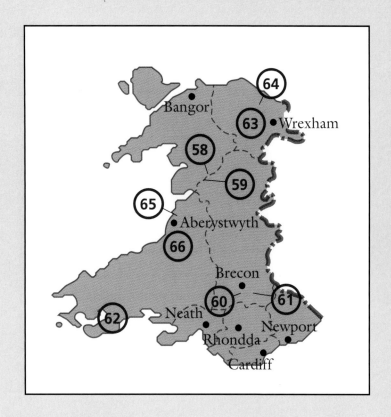

BANDIT COUNTRY

Mysterious bones and a bandits' burial site are features of this linear walk on the borders of Powys and Gwynedd.

1 Cars can be parked in the layby at Mallwyd (the finish of this walk). Take a bus from there to Cwm-Llinau, or you could complete a circle with an additional 3½ miles of road walking. Alighting from the bus, take the lane running uphill through the village, away from the A470 road and the River Dyfi. Pass the telephone box and village green on your left.

2 When you have gone past the entrance to Bryn-uchel Farm, you come to a fork in the lane – bear left here. Continue through a gate and across a bridge to climb up the pleasantly wooded valley. Head through another gate and cross the lane to continue up the valley along a rough track.

3 Across the valley you can see the windmills of Mynydd y Cemais on your right. Ignoring a track forking right to a gate, continue along the steady uphill track ahead. When the wall on your right turns right to run across the valley, maintain your direction up the valley, gradually climbing to a junction with another track coming from your left. Go right, with a fence on your left, to a gate giving access to the moorland.

4 Soon after you see the conifer plantation across the valley on your right, bear left uphill to the plateau. You come to a low, non-barbed wire fence, which is easy to cross. Head across the plateau and bear right into a valley occupied by the farmhouse of Craig-For.

5 Pass the farmhouse on your right and ignore a gate on your right immediately after it. Take the gate ahead to follow the farm track which bears left downhill. Cross a stream, then bear right with the track to cross another stream before rising to a cross-tracks at Bryn-glas.

6 Ignoring the track descending on your right, go ahead to walk with ruins, trees and a wall on your right. Also on your right is a fine view across the valley. Keep to this obvious track, ignoring tempting diversions uphill on your left. Take a gate ahead to continue round this hillside, with a fence on your right.

7 Come to a cross-tracks, where the private track on your sharp right gives permissive access to the burial mound of the Red Bandits at Collfryn. Ignore the track that bears left into the hills – instead, go ahead to reach the county boundary at a stream (Nant Gweinion). Ford the stream to enter Gwynedd, where the bridleway turns into an unclassified road. Bear right through a gate and follow the rough track around the hillside, keeping above the valley of the River Cleifion, and then head to Mallwyd.

FACT FILE

Distance 7 miles
Time 4 hours
Maps OS Landranger 125, OS Outdoor Leisure 23
Start Cwm-Llinau bus stop, grid ref 846077
Finish Mallwyd, grid ref 863124 (start by leaving cars here, bus from Mallwyd to Cwm-Llinau and walk back)
Terrain Moorland tracks
Nearest town Machynlleth
Parking Mallwyd
Refreshments The Brigands Inn, Mallwyd, shop and café at Mallwyd Garage
Public transport Bus no 518 links Mallwyd with Cwm-Llinau. It runs from Machynlleth, where there is a railway station. Tel 01970 617951 for times
Stiles None, but one non-barbed wire fence to cross
Suitable for Children, but not dogs as there are sheep in the area

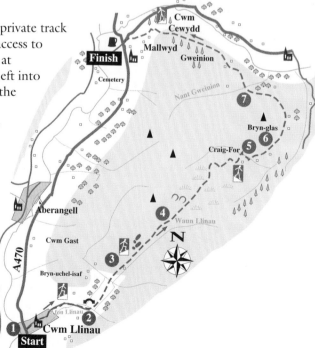

ALONG THE WAY

This walk takes you along part of the Dyfi Valley Way and Tony Drake's Cambrian Way. The area provided a sanctuary for the notorious Red Bandits of Mawddwy, who were wiped out in 1555. The 'monster' bones above the porch of St Tydecho's church were ploughed up when the porch was erected in 1641. The church was founded by St Tydecho, a nephew of King Arthur, in 520.

VIEWS FROM FRON GOCH

Ramble the gentle, rolling hills of old Montgomeryshire and admire Cadair Idris, Aran Fawddwy and the other hills of Southern Snowdonia from some superb viewpoints.

1 From the roundabout at Cemmaes Road, go along the A470 in the direction of Caersws, keeping the railway on your left. Pass the signposted Glyndwr's Way which comes down a lane on your right. Turn right over a stile to the left of a gate, to climb up the next signposted public footpath. This grassy track soon turns left to go through a gate then climbs gradually up the hillside. When you are joined by a fence on your right, look for a stile in it. Turn right to cross this stile and climb the hill, bearing very slightly left to continue over three more waymarked stiles in fences across your path.

2 Bear right to a stile in the far right corner of this field and cross it to join the lane (Glyndwr's Way). Go left to descend with this old cart road. Maintain this direction at a road junction to go with the Dyfi Valley Way to the hamlet of Darowen.

3 Walk past the church on your right; ignore the road that goes through Darowen on your right and the road that goes out of it on your left. Instead, take the lane ahead. This soon descends and deteriorates into a track. Cross two streams, one by a footbridge, before climbing as the track becomes a lane again. Pass the standing stone known as Maen Llwyd, which you can see in a field on your right. Follow the road to a junction on your right and turn sharply left into Tal-y-Wern. Cross the bridge and go straight on up the road which bears right.

4 Turn right through a gate to take the signposted path through woodland. Now make your way across a field above the stream, Nant Gwydol, on your right. Pass a farm on your left, then turn left through a gate and immediately right to descend with its access track to a road.

5 Go left along the road, then bear right with a waymarked path uphill, soon crossing a higher road. Eventually climb to a gate and go through it.

6 Bear right, following the waymarks, to go past a cottage on your left. Now turn right to follow a fence on your right. Descend to a stile in a fence near a corner that is shaded by trees.

7 Cross the stile and turn right to follow the fence on your right. Go straight on across a track and continue to a gate where a waymark arrow directs you to turn right before it and climb with a wall on your left. Continue climbing to the summit cairn of Fron Goch.

8 Cross the stile just below the summit, bear left and descend to a stile in the lower fence. Cross it and turn right to follow the waymarked path downhill. Cross the final field to a gate, go through it and turn right.

9 Go through gates to reach the road in Darowen and turn left. You soon go past the church on your left. Retrace your steps to where you joined Glyndwr's Way. Continue down the lane to Cemmaes Road.

FACT FILE

Distance 9 miles
Time 5 hours
Maps OS Landranger 135, OS Pathfinder 886
Start Cemmaes Road roundabout, grid ref 823044
Terrain Hill paths, old tracks, muddy woodland path
Nearest town Machynlleth
Parking Cemmaes Road
Refreshments A shop in Cemmaes Road
Public transport Buses Nos 518 (Machynlleth-Dinas Mawddwy) and 522 (Machynlleth-Newtown). Tel 01970 617951 for times
Stiles 10
Suitable for Older children, dogs on leads (sheep pasture)

ALONG THE WAY

Fron Goch, the hill above Darowen, is only 945ft (288m) high. Divert to the ancient earthwork on its summit, along an unofficial diversion which has been waymarked and had stiles erected with the permission of a friendly farmer.
The standing stone called Maen Lywyd is one of three that marked a 'Noddfa' or sanctuary. A hermit's cell used to stand beside it.

GENTLE GIANTS

This is probably the best, and certainly the quietest, way to visit the two highest Beacons summits. This circular route takes you through some of the National Park's finest scenery.

1 From the car, follow a wide path south to cross Nant Cwm Llwch by a narrow wooden bridge next to a shallow ford. Climb gently along a track to Cwm Llwch Farm, skirting it on the right by a slight detour in the route. Continue to climb up an obvious path through a field to a fence. Climb over a stile, which marks the boundary of National Trust land. From here, you can make a minor 'there and back' detour to view the Cwm Llwch waterfalls by following a narrow path off to the left. Follow the path, which becomes steeper now, noting a cairn on the right. From here a narrow path leads off left to the tarn of Llyn Cwm Llwch, from where you can easily rejoin the main path further on. Otherwise, continue ahead as the path ascends the lower slopes of Pen Milan, to meet the ridge of Craig Cwm Llwch.

2 When you reach the ridge, turn left along a sunken narrow path as it gradually sweeps around the vast bowl of Cwm Llwch, towards the first summit, Corn Du. After several hundred yards, keep a look-out on the right for the Tommy Jones Memorial. At the start of the ascent proper of Corn Du, the path becomes wider, steeper, and noticeably more eroded. The National Park has taken steps to stem this erosion by laying a stone 'pavement' leading to the summit.

3 From the top of Corn Du, follow a well-blazed trail across an obvious col to the broad flat top of Pen Y Fan, at 2,906ft, the highest mountain in South Wales. From here, the path descends north, steeply at first, down a badly eroded section, to meet the ridge of Cefn Cwm Llwch, where it levels off. If this steep bit is a little too daunting, you can avoid it by retracing your steps to the col, to pick up a narrow path contouring the north face of Pen Y Fan. This path joins the route at the foot of the eroded section. Follow it along the crest of the wide ridge as it gently swings north-east, and below the summit of the outlying hump of Allt Ddu. Don't be tempted to follow the two paths that lead off to the left, instead, keep to the main path as it starts a well graded

descent around the western side of Allt Ddu's northern slopes. After the path has swung to the right look for another path heading left directly down the hillside. Cross the Nant Gwdi stream over a footbridge and emerge at a car park next to the Cwm Gwdi army training camp. From here, follow the road downhill to a crossroads, where you turn left.

FACT FILE

Distance 7 miles
Time 3½ hours
Maps OS Landranger 160, OS Outdoor Leisure 11
Start/parking Gated field at end of lane, grid ref 006245
Terrain Clear paths/tracks. Some roadwork
Nearest town Brecon
Refreshments None on route
Public transport None
Stiles Two ladder stiles
Suitable for Dogs (must be kept under control) and older children

4 Follow the lane for about 1 mile as it winds past farms nestling under the Beacons. Cross the Nant Cwm Llwch stream by a stone bridge, and about 100yds later turn left into a narrow lane that leads back to the car.

ALONG THE WAY

Llyn Cwm Llwch is a small lake overshadowed by the giants of Corn Du and Pen Y Fan. Legend has it that a giant sleeps in the lake and, if awakened, will drown the Usk Valley below. The Tommy Jones memorial commemorates the tragic death of a five-year-old, who, in 1900, wandered up here and died of exposure.

The view towards Llyn Cwm Llwch from Corn Du

PEACEFUL WATERS

This walk connects two of the Beacons' most attractive reservoirs over limestone moorland seldom tramped by others.

1 From the end of the lane, head straight along a track, with the forest on your right and the round bump of Tor y foel behind you. After about a mile the track splits to the left at Pen Rhiw Calch. Continue dead ahead, the path dividing again after about 1½ miles. Take the left fork and follow the path as it makes its way towards the limestone quarries of Cwar yr Hendre and Cwar yr Ystrad, above the valley of Dyffryn Crawnon. Head towards the left of the workings, crossing the quarry road, and pick up a fence that runs up the side of the workings. Continue towards the end of the fence and from here bear right and make your way up the heathery slopes towards the summit of Cefn yr Ystrad. There are several large ancient limestone cairns on the summit.

2 From the summit of Cefn yr Ystrad, pick your own way to the southerly end of Cwar yr Ystrad quarry and head for the path that is clearly visible below. You can, if you wish, avoid the summit altogether by staying on the path along the valley bottom, to the right of the quarries, but if you do this you will miss the excellent views from the top. Turn left along the path, ignoring a path that goes off to the right after about ½ mile. After a further ½ mile take a right-hand

fork, making sure you don't wander too close to the old quarry workings on your right. Follow this path as far as the lane that leads from Merthyr Tydfil to Pontsticill Reservoir dam, and turn right.

3 Follow the lane to the Brecon Mountain Railway, past the dam, and continue ahead on the disused railway track. Follow the track along the easterly edge of Pontsticill Reservoir until you come to a metalled lane by the dam dividing Pontsticill and Pentwyn Reservoirs. Turn right up the lane, past the Dolygaer outdoor pursuits centre and the ruins of Dolygaer Farm. Where the lane becomes a track, follow it into the forest, up the valley of Cwm Callan, the Nant Callan stream below on the right. The track emerges from the forest over a stile, where it becomes a more distinct path and trends to the right across open moorland. To the left are the slopes of Bryniau Gleison. Keep with the path until it joins the one that you encountered earlier, coming in from the right. From here it is simply a matter of retracing your steps back to the car, with a final trot up to the top of Tor y Foel and back, to round off the walk.

This walk starts at scenic Pontsticill. the finish of the Brecon Mountain Railway

ALONG THE WAY

The quarries of Cwar yr Hendre and Cwar yr Ystrad, although unsightly, supply metallurgical limestone to the steelworks at nearby Ebbw Vale. The Brecon Mountain Railway runs from just north of Merthyr to Pontsticill, with plans to run it further up the valley. It is the only remaining working section of the Merthyr to Brecon railway, opened in 1863 and closed in 1962.

FACT FILE

Distance 11 miles
Time 5½ hours
Maps OS Landrangers 160/161, OS Outdoor Leisure 11
Start/parking End of lane from Talybont on Usk, grid ref 109188
Terrain Mostly good paths/tracks, one section not pathed, but navigation not difficult
Nearest town Brecon
Refreshments Brecon Mountain Railway Station, Pontsticill, but suggest you take your own
Public transport None
Stiles One
Suitable for Reasonably fit adults and older children

QUIET WATERWAY

The upper reaches of the Milford Haven Waterway take you away from
the busy ports into the rural hinterland of peace and tranquillity.

1 From Cresswell Quay walk north along the road, over Cresswell Bridge, taking the right-hand fork towards Martletwy. At Oakhill take the left-hand fork and remain on this quiet country lane until you reach the entrance to Baglan Farm. (Alternatively at Oakhill, take the right-hand fork along a lane to Yerbeston. Turn left opposite the farm and follow a green lane before turning left onto a tarmac road, then bear right at the bridleway sign. Cross fields, turn left at the road and left for Baglan Farm.)

2 Walk up the farm lane at Baglan and through Bush Farm before crossing open fields to Martletwy church.

3 Turn left at the church and walk along the country lane for a short distance. Turn right across open fields until you rejoin a quiet country lane which takes you into the village of Landshipping.

4 In Landshipping join The Landsker Borderlands Trail (look out for the distinctive waymarkers) and walk to Landshipping Quay. Just after the quay bear right onto the foreshore and follow the shoreline to Sam's Wood. The footpath then takes you up the wooded riverbank and across open fields to Coedcanlas. (Alternatively, instead of joining the foreshore at Landshipping Quay, continue along the lane and turn left. This route takes you across open fields to Prettyland Farm where you can join the quiet country lane to Coedcanlas.)

5 After walking past Coedcanlas Farm turn right across open fields to Garron. At Garron turn right onto the quiet lane which takes you into the village of Lawrenny. (Alternatively after crossing Garron Pill turn right along the foreshore and into Lawrenny Woods, an ancient woodland. This path leads to Lawrenny Quay and offers riverside views. Return to Lawrenny village along the lane.)

6 In Lawrenny it is well worth taking a detour to visit the viewing area beyond the church. This was the site of Lawrenny Castle and there are spectacular views across South Pembrokeshire.

7 In the village centre turn right towards Lawrenny Quay. Turn left on the outskirts of the village and cross open fields which follow the banks of the River Cresswell. Descend into Cresswell Quay through Scotland Wood and cross the stepping stones to return to your start point. (If there is a high tide, an alternative route is marked from Lawrenny, using quiet country lanes).

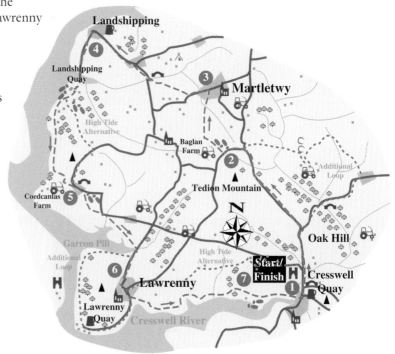

Cresswell Quay is now a tranquil backwater, but it was once a busy shipping centre

FACT FILE

Distance 10½ Miles
Time 4–5 hours
Maps OS Landranger 158, OS Pathfinder 1104 and 1080
Start Cresswell Quay, grid ref 051066

Terrain Easy undulating walking throughout with many stretches on level ground
Nearest towns Narberth, Pembroke
Parking There is ample room for free roadside parking at Cresswell Quay

Refreshments Bar snacks at The Stanley Alms, Landshipping. Tearoom at Lawrenny Village (limited summer opening only). Cresselly Arms, Cresswell Quay (no food).
Public transport None
Stiles 20–25, depending which route options you take
Suitable for Children

Looking west along Llantysilio Mountain from Moel y Gamelin

PEAKS OF PERFECTION

Choose a clear day and enjoy the dramatic views from Llantysilio Mountain.

1 From the village war memorial walk north-east for about 100yds then turn right onto a lane that winds up past Bryn Tirion house, beneath power lines. Beyond a lane joining from the left you reach a T-junction.

2 Go straight over, through a gate by a fingerpost for Moel y Gamelin. Follow the farm track uphill to a stile beside a tree-lined stream. Just above, a fingerpost points right. Walk up parallel to the stream at first, then angle half-left to a fence stile and over the next field to a track. Turn up right and reach open hillside at a gate. The track curves and climbs steadily through heather on the shoulder of Moel y Gaer, towards the flanks of Moel y Gamelin ahead. You soon arrive at a pass and cross-track.

3 Although you can avoid it if you want to, the climb to Moel y Gamelin's summit is highly recommended. Turn left up the rather eroded path, which is quite steep in places, to reach the little cairn at 1,896ft. To the east lies a dramatic view of Eglwyseg Mountain's great limestone escarpment above the Vale of Llangollen. As you return to the pass the other rounded summits of Llantysilio Mountain are set before you. In good weather you could opt for a direct traverse. From the pass descend south for a short distance and cross the stile by a gate over to your right. A narrow path, initially steepish, leads down over heather and bracken on the west

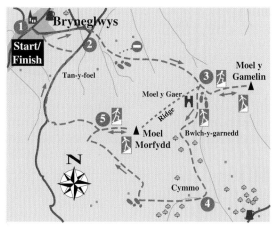

side of the valley to a fence and metal gate-stile at the edge of conifers. Follow the path down past the house, Bwlch-y-garnedd and walk down the tree-lined access track to a farm road.

4 Turn right and walk uphill to the entrance to Cymmo Farm, where you fork left through a gate. Above, the track crosses a stream ravine and gains height steadily. Keep straight ahead past an old corrugated shed and a derelict gate to reach a stile on open ground at the top of the slope. Turn right, parallel to a fence, towards the rounded bulk of Moel Morfydd. The fence curves round to a corner stile but you now angle left across to the next stile. Climb a steeper path through bracken, soon joining a track from the right. Continue walking uphill, with marvellous views over the Dee Valley. Once past a wooden post, turn right up the stony track onto Moel Morfydd (1,801ft). You are now at the western end of Llantysilio Mountain, where there are again spectacular views.

5 Return to the path intersection and carry on walking in a westerly direction on a gently climbing track which eventually drops to an unfenced road. Follow it downhill and take a footpath on your left opposite Tan-y-foel. This field path veers left through a gateway before cutting down right, under the power lines, and reaching the lane near Bryn Tirion. At the T-junction below turn left back to the start.

FACT FILE

Distance 7½ miles
Time 4 hours
Map OS Landranger 116
Start/parking Bryneglwys, grid ref 146473. Park carefully in village
Terrain Country lanes, fields and hill tracks. Two steep (though optional) climbs onto exposed hilltops
Nearest town Llangollen
Refreshments None on route but pub at Llandegla 5 miles north-east

Public transport GHA Coaches no 91 (Wrexham to Carrog) – one service Monday and Saturday only
Stiles Eight
Suitable for Older children, dogs on leads due to sheep

ALONG THE WAY

Llantysilio Mountain is really a mini-range in itself, ending to the east at the famous Horseshoe Pass and to the west at Carrog village in the Dee Valley. The walk skirts Moel y Gaer, an ancient hillfort. After an optional climb up the highest top – Moel y Gamelin – there's a long and gentle descent towards the Dee Valley before returning to the heights and climbing Moel Morfydd. The vast panorama takes in Snowdonia, the Clwydian Hills and the North Wales coast.

CROWNING GLORIES

Walk in the beautiful Clwydian Hills, topped with Iron Age hillforts.

1 Set off north-west from a footpath sign opposite the church. Walk past a toilet block, over a playing field and through a kissing gate and stile. Beyond a muddy hollow, a path over four fields with waymarked stiles (yellow chevrons) leads to a country lane at Cilcain Pumping Station. Keep straight on at a fork and follow the lane down and up to a sharp right bend at Tre-lan. Directly ahead another stile sets you on course over fields, passing to the right below Gors Farm. Bear slightly right and continue between waymarked stiles until you reach a farm track. Cross over and veer half-right downhill to find a stile in a little wooded valley, with a conifer plantation over to your left. Cross the shallow stream (taking care as it can be muddy) and turn left above it. Soon, angle diagonally uphill t o a lane crossing the Clwydian Hills range.

2 Turn left briefly, then go right over a stile and follow a low bank down the field. Cross one culvert and walk left alongside the

next to a field gate east of Plas-yw Farm. Climb straight up the hillside to a plantation corner, go through the gate and walk along the forest-edge track, keeping right at a fork. The track drops round past Firwood Farm and meets another one.

3 Turn up sharp left in an avenue of trees and pass a ruin. Further on the track disappears temporarily over pasture but soon continues round the western slopes of Moel Plas-yw with superb views over the River Wheeler valley, the Clwydian hillforts and the distant skyline of Snowdonia peaks. The pleasant green track eventually drops to a stile where a thin track forks up onto Moel Arthur (you can climb this as an optional extra if you wish). Turn right up the road past a gated road on the left and reach the pass. The gated road provides a shortcut back to Cilcain.

4 From the cattle grid and Moel Famau Country Park sign, turn left and walk up the steep hill to start the rugged ascent onto Moel Llys-y-coed. From here there is a tremendous panorama over the Vale of Clwyd and back to Moel Arthur hillfort.

5 After 1 mile on a hill track (part of Offa's Dyke Path) you reach a cross-track and finger post. Turn left and follow the delightful track round rough hillside and past the picturesque farmhouse of Plas-newydd where the lane becomes surfaced. There are good views all the way down over to Moel Famau and its summit tower. Keep right at junctions to come back to St Mary's church in Cilcain.

FACT FILE

Distance 8½ miles
Time 4 hours
Map OS Landranger 116
Start/parking St Mary's Church, Cilcain, grid ref 146652. Park carefully in village
Terrain Undulating field paths which can be muddy, good hill tracks and country lanes. One steep climb
Nearest town Mold
Refreshments White Horse Inn, Cilcain
Public transport Pied-Bull Coaches No 31 from Mold – three daily, Monday, Wednesday and Saturday
Stiles Numerous
Suitable for Older children, dogs on lead due to sheep

ALONG THE WAY

Isolated between the Vale of Clwyd, the Cheshire plain and the Dee estuary, the Clwydian Range offers exhilarating terrain for walkers. The rolling Clwydian Hills are crowned with superb examples of Iron Age hillforts. These hilltop settlements, originally defended by high, vertical ramparts and deep ditches, contained timber round-houses and probably granaries too. Moel Arthur is one of Clwyd's finest hillforts; although it covers only a small area, its precipitous southern slope **guarding the pass (Bwlch y Rhyfeinig) and massive ramparts to the north and east make it hugely impressive.**

THE FOSSIL FOREST

Follow a glorious cliff path from Aberystwyth to the fossil forest at Borth, then take the train or bus back. Splendid views across the Irish Sea give a romantic flavour as the sun sets.

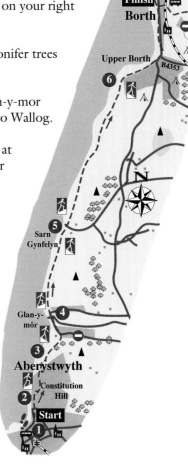

1 With your back to the railway terminus at Aberystwyth, cross the road by the pelican crossing, turn right, then turn left along Terrace Road. Pass the tourist information centre and the Ceredigion Museum on your right. Turn right along Marine Terrace to walk with the sea on your left.

2 Climb Constitution Hill by the zigzag path near the Cliff Railway. Just beyond its top station is a camera obscura. Continue by taking the path to the left of a cafe. Walk with a fence on your right and above the sea on your left.

3 Ignore a stile in the fence on your right. Go straight on through a plantation of conifer trees and descend to a road that gives access to a caravan site. Go left along this.

4 Cross a bridge over a stream and go straight on along the coast path, passing Glan-y-mor caravan site on your right. Follow the clifftop path as it gains height, then descends to Wallog.

5 The causeway of Sarn Gynfelin is on your left as you go ahead across a footbridge at Wallog, signposted for Borth. Continue with the sea on your left and a fence on your right to the war memorial overlooking Borth, straight ahead.

6 Descend to a road at the edge of Borth and walk with the sea on your left to its junction with the B4353 opposite the lifeboat station. Either continue along the beach or along the road parallel to it, keeping the sea on your left. The fossil forest appears about 2 miles after the lifeboat station.

7 Leave the beach just south of the fossil forest, where it is a short distance to the road on your right, before a golf course forms a wedge between the beach and the road. Turn right to cross the road and follow the signposted path across the golf course on the other side of the road. Cross the railway carefully and follow a causeway across the bog to the River Leri. Turn right over a stile to walk with the river on your left and a drainage ditch on your right.

8 Look across the bog to see St Matthew's Church on your right. Turn right to cross a stile and follow a path towards it. Bear right along a track which leads from the church to the railway. Cross the line carefully to reach the station platform for the train back to Aberystwyth. Buses also run to Aberystwyth from the main road beyond the station.

FACT FILE

Distance 9 miles
Time 5 hours
Maps OS Landranger 135, OS Pathfinder 926 and Outdoor Leisure 23
Start Aberystwyth railway station, grid ref 585816
Terrain Clifftop paths, beach or road, causeway over bog
Nearest town Aberystwyth
Parking Aberystwyth or Borth
Refreshments Aberystwyth or Borth

Public transport Trains run through Borth to Aberystwyth from Birmingham, Shrewsbury and Machynlleth. Tel 01267 231817 about buses
Stiles 4
Suitable for Older children

ALONG THE WAY

A few thousand years ago a fertile plain would have been laid at your feet. This is where the drowned land of Cantre'r Gwaelod (lowland Hundred) lies under the waves. Come at low tide to see the exposed causeway of Sarn Gynfelyn, while a fossil forest is exposed by spring tides north of Borth. Scientists date the fossil forest to about 3500BC.

TREGARON'S NATURE TRAIL

Walk with an old railway alongside the great bog of Cors Caron and pass a buried elephant!

1 Face the statue of Henry Richard, in front of Tregaron's Talbot Hotel. Turn round and go past the post office on your right. Take the bridge across the River Brennig and go right with the B4343 road, signposted for Pontrhydfendigaid. Continue for over 2 miles, passing a lake (Tyn-y-llyn) on your left. Look for the second layby and a stile on your left, just after the access lane to Maes-llyn.

2 Take the stile at the back of the layby and turn right along the disused railway line (now a nature trail). Reach an observation tower.

3 Retrace your steps to the layby and along the road back towards Tregaron, but take the first turning on your left. Climb with a lane to a house on your left and turn right when you are opposite it. You now follow a track that takes you to the next T-junction.

4 Turn right along a track which gives views over the bog on your right. Descend past Sunnyhill Farm to meet the main road again at a prominent beech tree.

5 Go left to return to Tregaron and the Talbot Hotel. Take a gate to the left of the hotel and pass the site of the elephant's grave. Turn right with the enclosed track and turn left through a gate. Cross a field to the next gate and bear right to a stile in the corner. Go ahead over a stile in the fence on your right, through a gate ahead and parallel with a lane on your left until a stile beside a gate gives access to it.

6 Fork right on a concrete farm access lane to Pencefn Drysgol. After ½ mile turn right over a stile beside a gate and walk with a fence on your right and over a stile in the corner ahead.

7 First cross a stream and go through a gate ahead, then bear right to go over a stile in the bottom right-hand corner of the next field. Turn left immediately to continue over a stile beside a gate and then bear right through two more gates and past a message on a tin shed which reads 'Croese i Dregaron, Cadwch Cymru'n Daclus' (Welcome to Wales, Keep Wales Tidy). Go right along a road which leads back into Tregaron and the Talbot Hotel.

FACT FILE

Distance 10 miles
Time 5 hours
Maps OS Landranger 146, OS Pathfinders 968 and 990
Start Henry Richard's statue, Tregaron, grid ref 681597
Terrain Roads, old railway line, lanes, tracks, field paths
Nearest town Tregaron
Parking Tregaron
Refreshments Tregaron
Public transport Buses nos 316, 585 & 589 from Aberystwyth, nos 581, 584, 588 & 589 from Lampeter and no 586 from Aberaeron (tel 01267 231 817 for times)
Stiles 8
Suitable for Children

ALONG THE WAY

Tregaron put George Borrow 'very much in mind of an Andalusian village overhung by its sierra'. While at the Talbot Hotel, at the start of this route, he 'experienced very good entertainment . . . had an excellent supper and a very comfortable bed', according to his *Wild Wales* (1862).

The railway came from Aberystwyth in 1866, crossing the bog north of Tregaron on the back of wooden faggots and bales of wool. It is now a nature trail, although the wildlife is not as exotic as the elephant that died here while on tour with a circus and now lies buried in a field at the back of the Talbot Hotel. Henry Richard was born here in 1812 and became known as the 'Apostle of Peace' before his death in 1888.

Looking over Cors Caron from nearby Sunnyhill Farm – see point 4

IRELAND

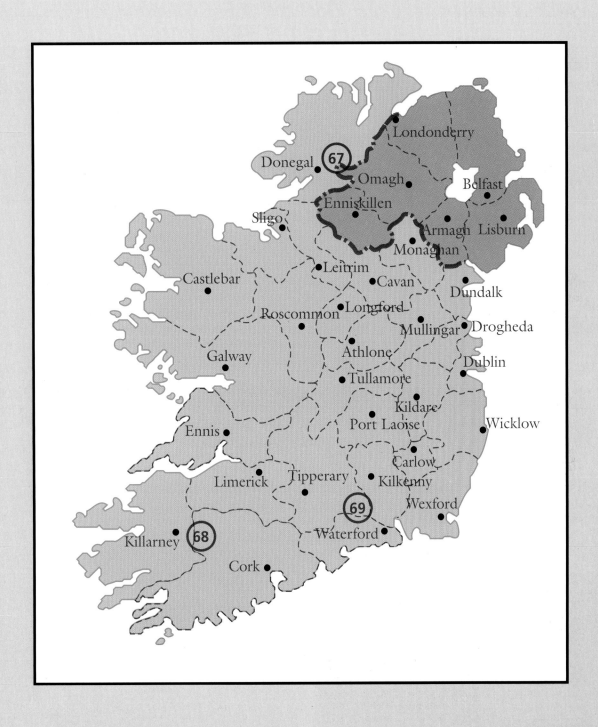

BOULDERY BLUE STACKS

The Blue Stack Mountains are broad, bleak, boggy and bouldery, but this walk is no real problem, providing you have clear weather. A short spur from the Ulster Way crosses Struell Gap and leads back down from the heights.

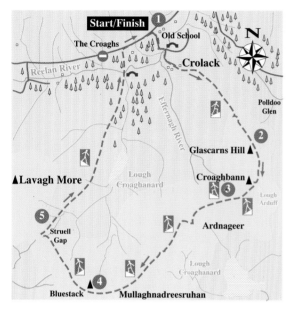

1 You need to locate the farm access road for The Croaghs by turning off the R253 road near Commeen, between Glenties and Ballybofey. Follow this narrow road and park by a disused national school. A track leads downhill nearby, crossing the Reelan River to reach Crolack. Keep left of the farm and gain the open slope beyond a sheep pen. Climb straight up the broad, boggy, bouldery slope to reach the summit cairn on Glascarns Hill.

2 Pass the summit and continue across a shallow gap. You will see little Lough Aduff on the broad top of Croaghbann before reaching the 2,100ft summit. Head westwards to descend, walking down great tilted slabs of granite to land on a rugged, bouldery gap near a pool.

3 As you walk across the gap towards the next summit, which is Ardnageer, you should look ahead and pick a way up a steep and rocky slope. You may need to use your hands in a couple of places, but an easier walk finally leads to the 2,118ft summit cairn. There is a slight gap beyond the main summit, followed by a slight ascent to a neighbouring height. On the shoulder of the hill is a prominent peak of pure quartz, and it's worth making a slight detour to this. Continue across another rugged gap before climbing to the 2,219ft summit of Bluestack.

4 This is the highest of the Blue Stack Mountains and there's a shelter cairn here, from where there are magnificent views of the Donegal Highlands. The descent north-west to the Struell Gap comes in two parts – a small lough lies in between two grassy slopes. There are only a few boulders and boggy patches on the way down to the gap, where you turn right at a prominent marker post.

5 The sparsely waymarked Ulster Way crosses the Struell Gap and leads north-eastwards across the boggy mountainside. You need to look well ahead to spot each marker post and there is no trodden path. A footbridge spans the Reelan River, which might otherwise prove to be impassable. Climb up the rugged pasture beyond and turn right along the farm access road to return to the national school at the start.

FACT FILE

Distance 9 miles
Time 6 hours
Maps OSI 1:50,000 Discovery Sheet 11
Start The Croaghs, grid ref 960942
Terrain Boggy, rocky and pathless uplands, where care is needed
Nearest towns Glenties and Ballybofey
Parking At the old national school
Refreshments Small pub off-route at Commeen
Public transport None
Stiles None
Suitable for Hardy hillwalkers and competent navigators

ALONG THE WAY

The Ulster Way is a 70-mile waymarked walking route through the rugged mountains of Donegal. The part crossing the Struell Gap is a spur from the main route. Further details can be found in a booklet called The *Ulster Way*, by Paddy Dillon, published by Walking World Ireland.

There are spectacular views from the 2,100ft summit of Croaghbann

CORK'S HILLS AND PLAINS

The Duhallow Way is a new trail in West Cork. A walk along it can be combined with an ascent of Caherbarnagh.

The view across to Caherbarnagh from the slopes of Claragh Mountain

1 To reach the start of the walk, drive away from Millstreet around the base of Claragh Mountain, through Croohig's Cross Roads and across Ahaphooca Bridge. Look out for a waymark arrow pointing left within yards and ask permission to park nearby. The arrow directs walkers up a farm access road, through gates, then uphill along a fenced path through fields to reach the higher moorland slopes.

2 The Duhallow Way turns right across the moorland slope at an electric fence, but you should continue straight uphill instead. When you reach the top of the steep, heathery slope, turn right to follow the broad moorland crest. There is a slight hump to cross, then a gentle rise leading to a prominent cairn at Stoukeen, which is just short of 2,000ft above sea level.

3 By heading roughly south-westwards, you can continue following the moorland crest. There is plenty of tussocky grass and squelchy ground, which could prove to be a problem in rain and mist. Clear weather is a distinct advantage when you are heading for the trig point on Caherbarnagh. The flat, boggy summit reaches an altitude of 2,239ft and views take in contrasting scenes of bleak hills and fertile plains.

ALONG THE WAY

The Duhallow Way runs from Bweeng Mountain to the Clydagh Valley and it forms an important link in a future waymarked coast-to-coast trail across Ireland. The Millstreet Country Park is a new countryside development that is well worth visiting.

4 Walk north-westwards, around the lip of a corrie, to reach the moorland hump of Glanaprehane. Continue more steeply downhill on drier, heathery ground until you run into a fence, where the vegetation changes from moorland to pasture. Turn right to pass close to Lough Murtagh, which is tucked away in a secret little hollow.

5 You are back on the course of the Duhallow Way, so look out for waymark arrows as you cross the outflowing stream from Lough Murtagh. The route continues to follow the fence eastwards, then later you climb gradually uphill across a stony slope to reach Gortavehy Lough.

6 After crossing a fence near the outflow of Gortavehy Lough, follow a track which leads above the lough, then continue to look out for markers along a boggy spur. Eventually you reach the electric fence noted near the start of the day's walk, so all you need to do is to turn left and retrace your steps down through the fields and along the farm access road back to your car.

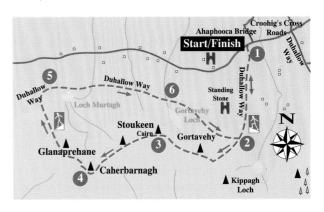

FACT FILE

Distance 8 miles
Time 5 hours
Maps OSI 1:50,000 Rambler Sheet 79
Start Near Ahaphooca Bridge, grid ref 220893
Terrain Easy on the lower slopes, but tussocky and boggy on top
Nearest town Millstreet
Parking Limited but ask permission at a farm near the start
Refreshments None on the route but plenty in Millstreet

Public transport Irish Rail and Bus Eireann serve Millstreet
Stiles A couple and some extra ones may be installed in due course
Suitable for Keen hillwalkers. Dogs are not permitted

HILL OF THE FAIRY CALVES

The Knockanaffrin ridge offers a fine walk high above the Nire Valley
and extensive views of mountain ranges across the south of Ireland.

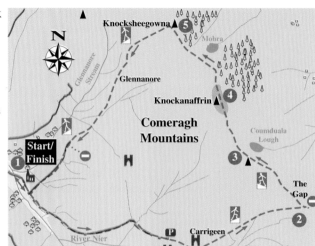

1 Drive into the Nire Valley and park near Nire church. If space is tight, continue along the road to a hillside car park. From the church, walk up the road to the higher car park, then follow a path which climbs uphill, parallel to the road, and goes through a gate. Waymark posts lead across a broad, boggy, hillside to The Gap.

2 A fence has been stetched across The Gap and you turn left to follow it uphill, climbing steeply up the ridge, which is made up of rock and heather. There is a fine traverse around the rop of Coumduala Lough, which occupies a deep and rocky hollow in the mountainside.

3 Continue up the next stretch of the ridge, looking ahead to the peak of Knockanaffrin. You can also turn around and admire the views across the broad, bleak and boggy Comeragh plateau. There are some large rocky blocks to cross on the way to the summit cairn at 2,478ft on top of Knockanaffrin. From here you can see the hump of Slievenamon, the Falty Mountains, Knowckmealdown Mountains, Blackstairs Mountains and Wicklow Mountains on a clear day, as well as the patchwork of the central plains.

4 Walk north along the rocky ridge, then bear a little to the left to descend steeply to a gap. A climb leads up the 2,181ft summit of Knocksheegowna, where a trig point is hidden behind a peak of rock. This is the Hill of the Fairy Calves – they are supposed to live beneath the waters of Lough Mohra, down the rugged mountainside.

5 Head west to start the descent down a rugged slope, drifting more to the south-west to enter old hill pastures. A path and track can be picked up which lead down to Glannanore, where a narrow road runs quickly down into the Nire Valley. At the bottom of this road, either turn right to end immediately at Nire church, or turn left to walk up the road to return to the hillside car park.

FACT FILE

Distance 9 miles
Time 5 hours
Maps OSI 1:50,000 Discovery Sheet 75, 1:25,000 Comeragh Mountains & Nire Valley Walking Guide
Start Nire church, grid ref 251139
Terrain Rugged and boggy mountain slopes
Nearest towns Clonmel and Dungarvan
Parking Nire church or further along the road

Refreshments Off-route at Ballymacarbry
Public transport None
Stiles A couple on the higher slopes
Suitable for Hardy hillwalkers

ALONG THE WAY

The Comeragh Mountains have twice been used as the venue for the Lowe Alpine Mountain Challenge, a two-day mountain marathon. Competitors use the 1:25,000 Comeragh Mountains map, which was specially produced for walkers. Information on walking routes in the area can be obtained from the Irish Tourist Board in London and from local tourist information centres.

The village of Henham, near Bishop's Stortford in Essex

SOUTH EAST

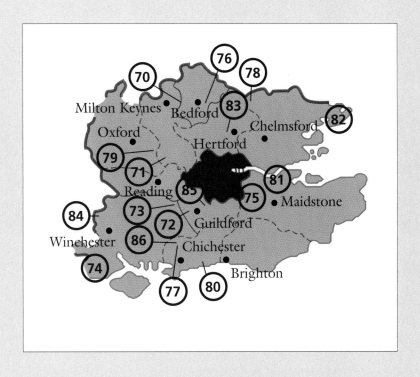

HOUSE BEAUTIFUL

The area around Ampthill is packed with interest and historical connections, and provided inspiration for John Bunyan. The countryside, high above the plain stretching to Bedford, gives good walking on a narrow band of greensand.

1 From the car park, it is worth visiting the dramatic ruins of Houghton House before setting off on the walk, so follow the signs up the track and on to the house. Walk back up the track to the sign pointing off to the left, and follow this, part of the Greensand Ridge Walk (GRW). This curves round on a gravelly drive, and you soon cross onto another concrete track leading to the gates of an underground reservoir.

2 From the gates turn right and, keeping close to the fence, walk gently downhill to another signpost, then go half-right to a stile. Continue down to a sign by the farm track, where you turn left to either brave the cattle grid or cross the stile. From here simply follow the surfaced track down to the road.

3 At the road turn right and follow it into Ampthill, passing the enchanting Church Square, to the old market square at the crossroads. At the junction cross into Woburn Street and follow this past the Queen's Head and on to Alameda Road. A gate leads through to the Alameda Walk, a lovely avenue of lime trees which brings you to a war memorial. Go through the gate and the scenery changes abruptly. The sandy track leads across a landscape of gorse and broom and onto a larger track crossing it. Follow this right and walk gently down to the road.

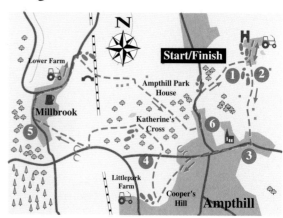

4 Turn right for a short distance until a way can be found on the left into Ampthill Park. Go through the car park and cross a stile into the park. Turn left to take the track as it leads round to climb to the war memorial and Katherine's Cross. Pause to admire the views and then follow the GRW signs down, and on to a stile by a small bridge. Cross this, the next field, and another stile into a narrow wood. Emerge onto a path between fences on the edge of farmland. Walk round, passing the farm on the left, and onto a track leading towards the tower of St Michael and All Angels Church, then drop down to the road in Millbrook.

5 Pass the Chequers and continue to the road junction where you turn right. Follow the road round until, just on a bend, a footpath sign and a stile lead to a field on the right. You soon reach the farm track that you walked past a few minutes before – this takes you over the railway and on to Park Farm. Walk to the left of the farm. A stile takes you into a field. Continue straight across to a stile leading into the park. After a few minutes' steep walking a good flat path leads along the edge. Follow this left (GRW signposts) to emerge onto the road just outside the town.

6 Turn left alongside the B530 and walk uphill until you reach the signs for Houghton House. Carefully cross the road and take the concrete track back along the ridge to the car park.

FACT FILE

Distance 6½ miles
Time 3½ hours
Map OS Landranger 153
Start/parking Houghton House car park off the B530, grid ref 037392
Terrain Easy walking on good paths. One steep climb; short, quiet road section.
Nearest town Ampthill
Refreshments Pubs and tea rooms in Ampthill and The Chequers at Millbrook
Public transport BR at Luton and Bedford, buses from Luton or Bedford. For Bedford tel

01234 228337, for Luton tel 01582 469369
Stiles Several
Suitable for Dogs and children

ALONG THE WAY

Houghton House dates from the 17th century and was built for the Countess of Pembroke. It is said to be John Bunyan's 'House Beautiful' in Pilgrim's Progress. In Ampthill Park, Katherine's Cross was erected in the late 18th century to commemorate Queen Katherine of Aragon's connections with the site.

MAUSOLEUM AND MANOR

Visit the villages of West Wycombe and Bradenham, both owned by the National Trust,
and walk along a long ridge that commands fine views.

1 From the car park, cross the grass on a well-worn path that leads uphill towards the Mausoleum and West Wycombe church. Pass to the left of these buildings and go through the churchyard to the National Trust car park. Make for the track to the left of Windyhaugh House. Follow this path along the ridge top, ignoring all turnings off.

2 Cross the road at Slough Bottom and continue straight on along the left-hand edge of two fields to another lane. Carry on along the right-hand edge of two more fields. Pass under an electricity cable and then turn right over a stile in the hedge. Cross a second stile and then bear left across the field. Make for a stile to the left of some trees – this leads you out to a road.

3 Turn right along this road to reach the A4010. Cross the road and turn left along a lane signposted to Loosley Row. Where the road bends left turn right to a stile in the hedge and then go left up the hill. At the top turn right and make your way down to a lane in Smalldean Bottom. Turn left along this lane, then go right through Smalldean Farm, following the edge of Park Wood, and across the fields to Bradenham.

4 Pass in front of the Manor House and turn left along a track. Fork right into a wood, following a path via intermittent waymarks through the wood, and down to the railway. Cross the railway with care and the A4010 with even more care, and continue across the field opposite. Turn left down the lane and follow it round to the right. Where the lane bends left continue straight on across the grass back to the start.

Start in the pretty village of West Wycombe

FACT FILE

Distance 9 miles
Time 3 hours
Maps OS Landranger 165 & 175
Start/parking West Wycombe Garden Centre, grid ref 827947 - ask for permission to park. Alternatively, use the National Trust car park at the top of the hill
Terrain Easy paths and tracks with five climbs. Mud after rain
Nearest town High Wycombe
Refreshments The Red Lion in Bradenham, pubs in West Wycombe, tea shop in West Wycombe Garden Centre
Public transport Bus services to West Wycombe and Bradenham, tel 01296 382000
Stiles Several, all easy
Suitable for Children and dogs (take care at railway and A4010)

ALONG THE WAY

The church at West Wycombe is Georgian and includes the famous Golden Ball. This was once fitted with a table and chairs and used for meetings of the Hellfire Club, a notorious men's club. The Mausoleum was built in 1752 to house the bodies of the club's members.

The Manor House at Bradenham was once owned by Isaac Disraeli, father of Benjamin Disraeli, who lived at Hughenden.

FACT FILE

Distance 8½ miles
Time 4 hours
Maps OS Landanger 186, OS Pathfinder 1225
Start/parking Puttenham Common car park off Suffield Lane, grid ref 919462
Terrain Fairly level; one stretch is along a busy country road

Nearest towns Aldershot, Farnham, Godalming
Refreshments Good Intent, Puttenham, The Cyder House Inn, Shackleford
Public transport None
Stiles Numerous
Not suitable for Young children and dogs

ALONG THE WAY

Puttenham Priory, described as a Palladian mansion, is privately owned and dates from the 1760s. The village well is in the adjacent churchyard of St John the Baptist, Puttenham. The last recorded use of this was in 1750; it was then forgotten, and only came to light again in 1972, when the covering collapsed into it!

THE FORGOTTEN WELL

An easy walk just south of The Hog's Back, this route takes in a common, an estate and two villages. Look out for a well, forgotten for over 200 years.

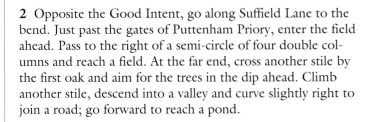

1 From the car park, cross the picnic area and join the track, going left beside the palings. You reach a green metal gate, and 75yds later fork right. Walk past a green and white house and descend to a crossing, where there is another green gate on the right. Go ahead, following the overhead lines, and pass a Woodland Trust enclosure. When you emerge onto open common, take the broad grass crossing track to the right: a mauve banded post identifies the crossing. Shortly after, by a notice board, turn right along the North Downs Way and descend to Puttenham village. Continue along The Street to the Good Intent, where you will turn right, but first visit the churchyard to see the village well.

2 Opposite the Good Intent, go along Suffield Lane to the bend. Just past the gates of Puttenham Priory, enter the field ahead. Pass to the right of a semi-circle of four double columns and reach a field. At the far end, cross another stile by the first oak and aim for the trees in the dip ahead. Climb another stile, descend into a valley and curve slightly right to join a road; go forward to reach a pond.

3 Turn right up the lane. Just past Lydling, turn left. Keep ahead over a stile and cross the grassland to an enclosed strip that leads to the road. Turn left into Shackleford, then right at the road junction towards Elstead.

4 Bear left at the telephone box up Grenville Road, and left again up Rokers Lane. Just after you have come level with the farm buildings away to the left, turn right at the marker post. You reach a four-way road junction, and take the farthest right, School Lane. At the bottom, turn right. Just beyond the

school, turn left along the path (295), staying beside a fence. Cross a stile under overhead lines and bear half-right, following the yellow arrow. In the second field, head for the trees at the far left corner. Cross the bridleway and walk through the belt of trees. Cross the next field to the buildings of Peper Harow, and follow the drive to St Nicholas Church; beneath the inscribed lych gate, there is a coffin rest.

5 Continue through the estate to an Edward VII letter box, then go through a wooden gate. Just beyond, turn left at the metal gate and aim for the far right corner, where a stile leads you out onto a narrow but busy country road.

6 Turn left, passing the farm entrance, and continue with care for ½ mile, ignoring a right junction, to the River Wey at Somerset Bridge.

7 Take the path (487) on the right before the bridge; this rises above the riverbank to continue in woodland, passing to the left of a wartime shelter. Cross a stream and go through Molly Mackerel's Farm to join the road. Turn left and, at the junction, keep left towards Cutmill.

8 Beyond the cluster of houses, the road crosses a stream on Gatwick Bridge. After 125yds, by the drive leading to Cuttmill Cottage, bear half-right along the bridleway. At the end of this, cross a track and enter the grounds of Cutt Mill House; skirt the lake anti-clockwise to reach the drive.

9 Turn right, staying outside the wall. At the end you join a path which climbs through woodland to reach another drive. Keep ahead, curving left to pass the main house, Rodsall Manor, and Rose and Briar Cottages. Take the left fork 30yds later, and after a further 150yds, go up the stepped path on the left to emerge opposite the car park.

LINE OF DEFENCE

Much of this very pleasant walk is along the towpath of a restored canal with a fascinating history.

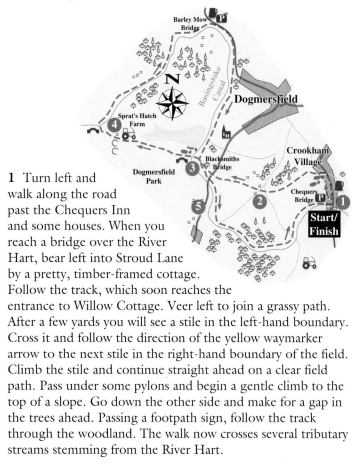

1 Turn left and walk along the road past the Chequers Inn and some houses. When you reach a bridge over the River Hart, bear left into Stroud Lane by a pretty, timber-framed cottage. Follow the track, which soon reaches the entrance to Willow Cottage. Veer left to join a grassy path. After a few yards you will see a stile in the left-hand boundary. Cross it and follow the direction of the yellow waymarker arrow to the next stile in the right-hand boundary of the field. Climb the stile and continue straight ahead on a clear field path. Pass under some pylons and begin a gentle climb to the top of a slope. Go down the other side and make for a gap in the trees ahead. Passing a footpath sign, follow the track through the woodland. The walk now crosses several tributary streams stemming from the River Hart.

2 Follow the track round to the right to cut between several isolated houses. Walk up the track between hedges and trees; after a few yards climb the stile in the left bank. This takes you into a paddock, where you head diagonally right towards a stile among some conifer trees. Cross two more stiles in quick succession and then follow a narrow path between wire fences. After about 75yds it bears sharp right to another stile. Follow the clear path diagonally across the field. Soon the path curves right beneath some power cables and runs straight to the road. Cross the road and join a narrow path that cuts between houses. You soon emerge onto a track running along the edge of some dense woodland. It curves to the left and then leads up to Blacksmiths Bridge.

3 As you approach the bridge turn right and follow the towpath of the Basingstoke Canal. After little more than 1 mile you come to Barley Mow Bridge. Continue on the towpath beyond Stacey's Bridge and Baseley's Bridge and eventually you come to Sprat's Hatch Bridge. Leave the towpath at this point and go up the bank to a stile.

ALONG THE WAY

Basingstoke Canal, completed in 1794 and 37 miles long, was originally intended to be a major commercial route between London and North Hampshire. However, its potential was never fully exploited. The owner of Dogmersfield Park, Sir Henry Mildmay, refused permission for the waterway to cross his land. As a result the Basingstoke Canal Company devised an expensive loop around the estate's northern boundary. The walk follows this route.

During the Second World War the canal formed part of a line of defence between the east and west coasts to hamper enemy invasion. The remains of old tank traps can still be seen. Tundry Pond covers about 20 acres and was originally part of Dogmersfield Park.

The Basingstoke canal was used as a defence during World War II

Turn left, avoid a path on the right running through the bracken, and follow the clear path that takes you to Sprat's Hatch Farm.

4 Join a drive and follow it as it curves left. Bear right opposite the farm gate and follow a narrow path across the field. Dogmersfield Park can be seen on the right. Cross a stile in the boundary, turn left and head for the field corner. Cross another stile and then swing right to follow a path alongside Tundry Pond. Make for the trees and, when you reach them, veer right to follow a clear path that takes you back to Blacksmiths Bridge. Cross the bridge, then bear immediately right to rejoin the towpath. Go under the road bridge and past a huge overhanging oak tree. On the opposite bank is an unusual Dutch-style house set in its own spacious grounds.

5 The canal meanders between bursts of light woodland which then becomes thicker. Further on there are the remains of an old bridge. Pass between more lines of trees to reach the old wharf at Chequers Bridge.

FACT FILE

Distance 6½ miles
Time 2½–3 hours
Map OS Landranger 186
Start/parking Chequers Bridge just south of Crookham Village, grid ref 792516
Terrain Mainly field paths, long sections of towpath
Nearest town Aldershot
Refreshments The Chequers Inn, Crookham Village, The Barley Mow, Dogmersfield
Public transport Altonian Coaches operates service 207 via Crookham Village. BR station at nearby Winchfield
Stiles A few
Suitable for Children and dogs

SMUGGLER COUNTRY

For much of this fascinating walk you are following paths and tracks once used by smugglers.

1 From the car park turn left and walk along Chapel Lane. Follow it until you see a turning on the right to St John the Baptist Church. Follow Church Lane and then swing right opposite the church onto a stony track. Walk alongside the cricket ground and beyond Burley primary school you come to the road opposite the Moor Hill House Hotel. Turn left and follow the road for about 130yds. Bear right at the car park sign.

2 Follow the stony track, ignoring the turning on the right and continue beyond a Forestry Commission car-free area barrier. Follow the clear path in a southerly direction. Drop down the bank between carpets of bracken and then curve right towards a white cottage, passing under some power lines. When you draw level with the cottage, veer left and then right after about 75yds to join a path through the bracken. Further on it merges with another track. Eventually you reach a fork just before some power lines. Veer left and follow the path up the slope and then down the other side. Follow the way down to the route of an old railway line which ran between Brockenhurst and Poole.

3 Turn right and walk along the track bed. If it is wet in places you can use the parallel paths. Continue to the road bridge, bear right and follow the road for a short distance before veering half-left under another line of power cables.

Head towards some trees and pass through them. Continue across open heathland and keep to the main path through the gorse. Aim for another line of trees and to the right you will see a white cottage set in the woodland. The long ridge to the east is defined by Burley Beacon, Burley Hill and Castle Hill. Go through a gap in the trees and the sunken path becomes sandy. You can see several white houses among the trees on the right. Drop down quite steeply and then climb up the other side. The path is deeply scarred here.

4 At a fork just before some power lines, veer right and head for the trees. Make for the top of Castle Hill and from here there are magnificent views over the New Forest. As you reach the trees, there is another fork. Bear right to a track and then turn right. Follow it between oak and holly trees, past a settlement of houses. Just beyond them turn left over a stile. Follow the path as it winds through the delightful woodland. Pass a footpath on the left and continue to cross a rustic footbridge. Follow the path as it bends right and then left. Walk along to the gates at the entrance to Burley Hill House. The road is in front of you.

5 Turn right and follow the road for about 50yds. Take the waymarked path to Burley. The path runs parallel to the road. Walk through the village, turn left at the Queen's Head and the car park is on your left.

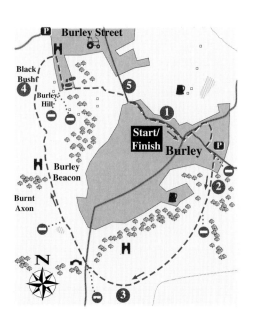

FACT FILE

Distance 5 miles
Time 2 hours
Map OS Landranger 195, OS Outdoor Leisure 22
Start Burley, grid ref 212032
Terrain Mostly level forest and heathland paths and tracks
Nearest town Ringwood
Parking Car park off Chapel Lane
Refreshments Queen's Head, Burley. Burley Manor Hotel is open to non residents and offers morning coffee, teas and bar snacks
Public transport Wilts and Dorset operate several bus services to Burley, including 105, 116, 118 and X1
Stiles Only a couple
Suitable for Children and older people. Dogs on a lead

ALONG THE WAY

The Queen's Head in Burley used to be a meeting place for smugglers who used the network of paths and tracks. The dense woodland provided refuge from the revenue men. Burley Beacon features in various legends. Dragons were once said to stalk this remote part of the forest.

SEVEN TO ONE

Both Sevenoaks and One Tree Wood are misnomers, but this walk through a well-wooded part of Kent sees relics of damage from the great storm of October 1987

1 From the car park, walk past the tourist information centre to the main street and turn left. Beyond the shops is the entrance to Knole Park. Once through the gate, turn right over the grass into a large dry valley, where you are likely to see deer and woodpeckers. Follow this valley and at the end climb to a drive, near an exit gate from the park.

2 Turn left along the surfaced drive and when it splits, fork right onto Chestnut Walk, following the Greensand Way sign. There are magnificent views of the park all around.

3 After ½ mile you reach a cross-paths, where you turn right to leave the park, following the Greensand Way signs. Cross the road, go through a small wood, and along the right side of a field. Leave the field over a stile, turn right for a few yards and then left over another stile. The path leads along the edge of a field, with great views across East Sussex. At a narrow road, cross over and go straight ahead along the track, then fork left to pass White Rooks farm. When you reach a narrow road turn left for a few yards and then right over a stile, along the edge of the wood. After two stiles, pass a spring and an isolated house built of stone and hung tiles. Follow the track beyond here, until a sandy, stony track leads off to the left.

4 Turn sharp left here and climb gently up over the top of Wilmot Hill. Keep straight ahead as far as a narrow road. Turn left and after a few yards turn right on the path into the woods, soon emerging by a large open field on the left.

5 Just past the open field is One Tree Hill, but keep ahead, following the wooden fence on the left. Where the track bends right, go straight ahead, passing beneath the fence. Follow the grassy path to an open area and a granite seat, with views south from the top of the Greensand scarp. From the seat walk west along a grassy path, to the car park area and out onto the road.

6 Turn right for a few yards, and then turn left following signs to Riverhill and Sevenoaks, along Fawke Wood Road. This leads straight through to a gateway into Knole Park. The drive splits and you take the major fork to the right, passing Keepers Cottage, then head across the golf course to come alongside the house. Descend to a small valley where a left turn brings you up to the house. From here, walk over the top of Echo Mount Hill and then head straight down into the dry valley, a few hundred yards to the right of the main entrance used at the start of the walk. Here you will see another of the deer-proof gates, and beyond this a sur-faced path leads up to the car park and the town centre.

FACT FILE

Distance 8 miles
Time 4 hours
Maps OS Landranger 188, OS Pathfinder 1208
Start/parking Sevenoaks town centre car park next to tourist information centre, grid ref 532546
Terrain Undulating along well-marked paths and tracks
Nearest town Sevenoaks
Refreshments A wide choice in Sevenoaks but nothing on the route
Public transport Sevenoaks is well served by both bus and rail
Stiles Several small stiles, but no real obstacles
Suitable for Children and dogs

Knole House is set in a magnificent deer park, which forms a beautiful setting for this walk

ALONG THE WAY

Knole House stands on a small hill – a knoll, hence its name – and is situated in the heart of a magnificent deer park. Dating from 1456, it is built of local ragstone and was extended by Henry VIII. Queen Elizabeth gave it to her cousin Thomas Sackville, whose descendants still live here. Knole, the largest private house in England, is managed by the National Trust, and is open to the public from April to the end of October. The park is open all year round.

DOVES AND DUCKS

Starting at the village of Willington, with its National Trust Tudor dovecote, this mainly flat route visits the modern Willington Lock.

1 Starting from the dovecote, walk past the church, turn left and head along the village street. At the white cottage go right into Balls Lane. Follow this the A603, and walk left alongside the road for a few hundred yards to Wood Lane. At a fork in the main road is an attractive old beamed cottage, The Old Forge.

2 Although surfaced, the lane carries virtually no traffic and once beyond the nurseries gives easy walking for almost 1 mile. Pass Hill Farm Cottages and go on to Hill Farm itself, where a bridleway leads off parallel to the wooded ridge.

3 The broad, grassy track leads straight across farmland. It's easy to follow by the line of single trees stretching away southwards. Cross two culverts, the first by a concrete bridge, and the second by a wooden one. The trees are popular hunting sites for kestrels and you are likely to see them hovering here.

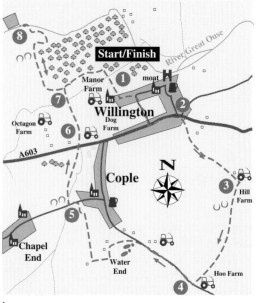

4 At the road, turn right past Hoo Farm and continue for about ½ mile until you are just past Middle Farm, where a footpath goes diagonally across a field on the left. Go through a gap in the hedge and alongside the garden of a thatched cottage, to the road. Turn briefly left, then right onto the bridleway (this has a County Council order on it to downgrade to a footpath, so it may be signposted as such). Whatever its designation, it is a pleasant gravel track giving easy, dry walking to a gap in the hedge and a tumbledown barn, where it changes direction to run alongside a hedge. This again gives good walking with excellent views to the huge airship sheds at Cardington.

5 At the playing fields a dog-leg leads onto the road. Turn left for a few hundred yards, cross a bridge and take the bridleway next to the stream.

6 Cross the road and take the track through Dog Farm, past the bungalow and into open countryside again. Cross another small stream and the way leads towards a group of trees. Just inside the trees, you reach the now disused Bedford to Sandy railway line. For the longer walk take a left turn here. This takes you to the River Ouse at Willington Lock, and is well worth the effort. However, you can turn right here and follow the track back to the village.

7 Go over the quarry access road and continue half right down the gravel track. Follow the perimeter of the site, all the while on a good path, to a stile that leads onto another stony track. This leads straight to the river, then turns alongside to the modern weir and lock. Here a flight of steps leads down to staging at river level, or as sometimes in winter, below the water.

8 Retrace your steps but, instead of crossing the stile, take the signposted bridleway between the hedge and the fence. This soon leads via a gap in the hedge to the gravel track and then the old railway. Pass through the gate and walk past the point where you got onto the line. Now continue along the track to a new gate. Turn right and again cross the stream. Continue up the track for a few minutes and back to the dovecote.

FACT FILE

Distance 6 or 7½ miles
Time 3½–4 hours
Maps OS Landranger 153
Start/parking Beside Willington Dovecote at Church End, grid ref 107500
Terrain Bridleways and field paths, some quiet lanes
Nearest town Bedford
Public transport BR at Bedford. Buses 178 and 179 – for details tel 01234 228337
Refreshments Pubs at Willington and Cople
Stiles Only one
Suitable for Children and dogs

ALONG THE WAY

The Tudor dovecote has 1,500 nest holes and 'stables' – you can visit these – Mr Askew, who lives in the house next door to the dovecote, has the key. Willington's also has a fine old church, while Cople's dates back to 1450 and contains many fine brasses.

GOOD SPORTS

Take a sporting walk across a golf course and past some of the most famous polo pitches in the country. There are also fine open views across Cowdray Park to the sandstone hills further north and to the South Downs.

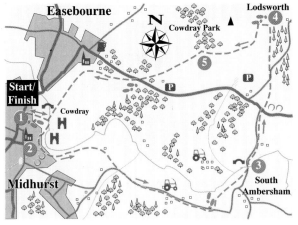

1 From the car park walk along the track towards the old house, but just before the bridge over the river turn right to follow the riverside path. As it bends round to the left you may want to take a slight detour up the steep slope to look at the low wall remnants of Midhurst Castle.

2 Follow the river, cross a stone bridge over a tributary of the Rother and turn left beyond the cottage. The path climbs for a short distance as the river gradually bends away to the left. There are magnificent views across the park from this elevated position. Keep straight ahead to Balls Barn and then emerge on a narrow road, passing Great Todham and then Little Todham. At a slight bend in the road, go left along the field margin parallel to the road, and at a solitary oak tree turn left on a track across the field to walk down to the river. Against the skyline ahead is the mast on the top of Bexley Hill Common. Turn right and follow the river to the narrow road.

3 At the road turn left, cross the stone bridge, and walk along the road until you reach the A272. Cross over and take the path through the trees to a small road. After 100yds, where the road bends slightly, go left, following the public bridleway along the edge of the woods.

4 At the northern end of the woods, turn left along the field margin. After 200yds, go left again to walk alongside a small wood to a stile and a signpost pointing across the open sloping field. In front of you at the bottom of the slope is Steward's Pond. Pass to the left of this small lake, through the gate, and continue up a slight hill on a grassy path between trees. Just before the top of the slope fork left to emerge onto the golf course.

5 Head to the left of two greens and a wooden shelter, then follow the rough on the right of the eighth fairway, beneath an oak tree, hoping that no one with a bad slice comes up behind you! Walk past two greens and you then come out onto the road. Turn right, and by the 18th tee, cross the road and head diagonally down across the field to the right of the polo pitches. This path leads out to the buildings near the church of Easebourne, where a left turn along the stony track leads you back to the Cowdray ruin and into Midhurst.

Cowdray Park is home to one of our most famous polo teams

FACT FILE

Distance 6½ miles
Time 3 hours
Maps OS Landranger 197, OS Pathfinder 1266
Start Car park at the end of the main street in Midhurst, grid ref 887217
Terrain Gentle
Nearest town Midhurst
Parking At the eastern end of the High Street
Refreshments Pubs and cafés in Midhurst, but nothing on the walk
Public transport Bus services to Midhurst from Guildford, Chichester or Petworth
Stiles Several, but no difficult ones
Suitable for Children and dogs

ALONG THE WAY

Cowdray House, which you pass early in the walk, is still lived in by the Cowdray family and is not open to the public. Look out for the cottages and farm buildings belonging to the estate – they all have yellow doors and window frames. The ruins of the old house, which was destroyed by fire in 1793, are open to visitors but only from April to September. There is a museum here as well. The beautiful park is the home of one of England's most famous polo teams.

ROUND THE MANOR

This pleasant walk takes you past the beautiful grounds of Audley End House and also offers the opportunity to explore picturesque Saffron Walden.

1 From Audley End station turn right at the end of the approach road and walk downhill to the B1383. Turn left then right into Wendon Road (signed to Saffron Walden). Cross the River Cam and, at the end of a small spinney, bear left into a footpath leading along the edge of this. Go through the yard of Abbey Farm, turning sharp left into a driveway and pass another drive to St Mark's College on the left. Continue uphill, past the white painted cottages of Audley End, and turn left at the end to walk to the main entrance of Audley End House.

2 Continue along the road and cross the bridge. Stop to admire the views of the house and grounds, then walk up to the B1383. Continue for about 350yds before turning right down a track next to the perimeter wall of the mansion grounds (signed to Home Farm). Cross the river again and take the path leading off to the right, just after the left-hand bend . Follow this between the wall and a stream, go through the kissing gate and continue through a meadow, cross a second meadow and pass through another kissing gate. Go between two fences, then over a bridge and walk up to the latch gate to leave the estate grounds.

3 Go straight ahead along Abbey Lane, passing some almshouses, until you reach the High Street. Turn left, then take the second right into Church Street and turn left again to walk into the grounds of the Church of St Mary the Virgin. For the shorter walk, retrace your steps to the gate at the end

of Abbey Lane. From inside the park, take the path leading left at the fork, walk uphill and leave by another latch gate. Bear right into a road leading downhill, back towards the main entrance of the house. Just before this, turn left and retrace your steps through the village back to the start.

4 For the longer walk, turn left from the castle ruins into Little Walden Road and then bear left into Catons Lane. Walk downhill past the football club, con tinuing onto a footpath and follow this uphill. Turn left into a drive and, after a few yards, turn right onto a footpath, signed to Springwell. Follow this, walking beside a ditch, continue uphill and go through a gap in the hedge. Go straight on, then the path turns sharp left to go downhill along a track under the power pylons. Watch out for the deer on the right as you continue to Springwell, pass the farm buildings and emerge onto the B184 road.

5 Turn right and, after a few yards, take the footpath to the left, opposite Springwell Nursery. The path soon veers left, down through some bushes to a stile. Cross this and head across a meadow by the River Cam. Leave it by a kissing gate next to St Mary's Church in Little Chesterford and walk down the road, bearing right into a track (don't cross the river). Continue along a footpath next to the hedge, cross another footpath and turn left into Great Chesterford village. Con tinue down the road, passing The Plough and the 13th century All Saints' church, and then join the B1383. Turn left, then bear right to walk up the approach road to the station.

FACT FILE

Distance 4½ miles or 7 miles
Time 2½ hours or 4 hours
Map OS Landranger 154
Start/parking Audley End station, grid ref 517362
Terrain Easy going, but slightly hilly on the longer route
Nearest towns Bishop's Stortford, Cambridge
Refreshments Tea rooms next to post office at Audley End and The Fighting Cocks near Audley End station. Pubs in Saffron Walden; The Plough in Great Chesterford

Public transport British Rail Liverpool Street to Cambridge service. Great Chesterford station is closed on Sundays. Eastern National Bus 301, Bishop's Stortford to Saffron Walden (not Sundays). Cambus Route 22, Cambridge to Saffron Walden via Great Chesterford (not Sundays). On Sundays, Hedingham Omnibuses service 102/103, Cambridge to Saffron Walden via Great Chesterford
Stiles One, easy
Suitable for Children, dogs on leads, elderly on the short walk

ALONG THE WAY

Audley End House is open from Easter to the end of September. There is also a miniature railway which runs steam on Sundays. In Saffron Walden, the 13th century Church of St Mary boasts a steeple almost 200ft high, added in 1832. The castle ruins are all that remain from the original building; there are many 16th and 17th century buildings in the town centre and Great Chesterford dates back to Roman times.

RIDGES AND BEECHWOODS

Ideal for late autumn, this walk explores the beechwoods and farmland around the parish of Fawley in the extreme south-western corner of Buckinghamshire. The climax of the walk is the superb open ridge running south from Stonor.

1 From Middle Assendon head east along the lane, which is signposted to Fawley. Bear right onto the Oxfordshire Way, crossing the Buckinghamshire–Oxfordshire boundary at the top of the first ridge. Continue along the track by Pond Cottage, then go left along the field edge (path 30).

2 Cross a lane and then turn right at a T-junction to go past a private zoo. Just after the track bends right, bear left downhill by a fence through the wood and continue across two fields to the A4155.

3 Turn sharp left back up the field to the opposite corner and follow a waymarked path up through the wood to reach a road. Continue along this road. Turn left just after The Cottage (the last house), then go between fences to reach the village of Fawley.

4 Turn right through the village along the ridge top, past the village hall and green. Later you pass the Walnut Tree restaurant. Just before a right-hand bend, turn left onto a path between hedges by a hidden public footpath sign.

5 At Bosmore Farm, turn right along a lane past a duck pond. After you pass the last house turn left across two fields, then go right along the drive to Coxlease Farm.

6 Turn left along the ridge track at the farm buildings. The path bends right to a wood. Follow it through the wood and down a field to the B480. Turn left along this road back to the start.

FACT FILE

Distance 7 miles
Time 3 hours
Map OS Landranger 175
Start Middle Assendon, grid ref 739857
Terrain Well defined paths and tracks. Three climbs
Nearest town Henley
Parking In Middle Assendon near the Rainbow in a long layby
Refreshments The Rainbow in Middle Assendon. The Walnut Tree in Fawley
Public transport BR to Henley (The Oxfordshire Way links the walk to Henley)
Stiles Several, easy
Suitable for Children and dogs

ALONG THE WAY

There are plenty of splendid sights to enjoy on this walk – the view over Middle Assendon from the top of the first ridge is superb, as is the panorama across to Maidensgrove from the ridge running south from Stonor.

Fawley is a linear settlement built on top of a north-south ridge. The church was restored in 1883. A recent addition is a small stained glass window by the late John Piper who lived at Fawley Bottom. In the churchyard are two mausoleums, one built for the Freemans who lived at Fawley Court, by the Thames.

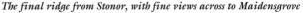
The final ridge from Stonor, with fine views across to Maidensgrove

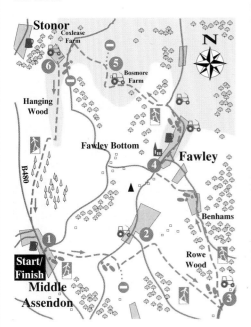

SAFE HAVEN

This downland circuit starts and ends at the foot of Cissbury Ring and visits the flint workings on the ring, one of the earliest industrial sites in Britain.

1 From the car park go through the gate and straight ahead to the information board. Walk up the steep hill and bend round to the right along a worn path, which has a few wooden steps higher up, and then a concreted section just before the most eroded patch near the stile. Beyond the stile continue up the smaller concrete steps, before turning right along the rampart. Follow it round the western end, passing the old flint workings which contain dense patches of vegetation in the sheltered hollows. New views along the coast open up every few yards. When you reach the main cross track, coming from the right, turn left and walk up to the triangulation point. Views from the top are magnificent – to the east is Beachy Head, while to the west is the Isle of Wight. Turn right at the trig point and at the rampart go left up the steps and walk along it to complete the 1-mile circuit of the Ring. Descend the concrete steps and go back to the gate near the car park.

2 Turn right along the stony track and pass to the left of a large barn. Walk on downhill, for about 1 mile, and where the path splits, take the left fork and climb up to the cross paths. Turn left along a bridleway and follow this, downhill at first and then with a long steady climb up towards a minor road.

3 Where the path is adjacent to the minor road, keep straight ahead on the South Downs Way. Views have opened up to the east to the quarry for Shoreham cement works and the mast further east along the Downs, across the Adur Valley. At a flint pebble memorial to Walter Langmead, a Sussex farmer, there is a cross-paths, but just keep straight ahead. Follow the South Downs Way for 1 mile towards Chanctonbury Ring, whose woodland looks rather sparse since the storm damage of October 1987.

4 Before you reach the Ring, at a major cross-route, where a path goes steeply down to the right through the woods and down the scarp, turn left along a stony track. This splits almost immediately, but ignore the right fork and go straight ahead in a southerly direction. The last views north to the Weald are behind you and ahead are the wave-like undulations of the dip slope with the sea in the distance. A few trees on the right provide a little shelter. A track comes in from the right, and beyond a small wood the view opens out again to Cissbury and the end of the walk. Walk straight on past a cross-track and then a cross-path to return to the car park.

FACT FILE

Distance 8 miles
Time 3½–4 hours
Maps OS Landranger 198, OS Pathfinder 1306, 1287
Start Cissbury Ring, grid ref 139086
Terrain Good paths and tracks all the way, with one steep climb which can be slippery after rain
Nearest town Worthing
Parking A small National Trust car park at the foot of Cissbury Ring. Reach it by leaving the A24 five miles north of Worthing and driving through Findon
Refreshments In Findon
Public transport Buses along the A24
Stiles One wooden one
Suitable for Older chldren

ALONG THE WAY

Cissbury Ring is an Iron Age hillfort covering 65 acres. There was a tribal capital here in about 300 BC, though the site had been used as early as 3,000 BC. For the Neolithic people flint was essential because it produced a cutting edge, vital for knives, scrapers and arrow heads. Its archaeological interest as well as its steep slopes enabled the Ring to escape the widespread ploughing of the Downs, which took place after the Second World War. A rich variety of wildlife remains, including eight species of orchid, field fleawort, snakes, lizards, kestrels and skylarks.

ANCIENT AND MODERN

Glorious countryside is all around you on this walk past Neolithic relics, Norman churches and within sound of the noisier modern structure, the M20.

1 Detling village has several interesting old houses, a pub, a shop and the Norman Church of St Martin of Tours. Walk along the road from the church to the A249. Cross the road – slightly to the right is the minor road, Harpole Lane. Follow this for 100yds, then turn left along the track by the first house. After a few hundred yards, where the track bends left, go straight on over the stile and past some huge oak trees to reach Boxley church.

2 Parts of the remarkable Church of St Mary and All Saints date back to Norman times – it is worth stopping here for a look. From the church follow the line of cobbles which is thought to be the route of an old Roman road, but will certainly lead straight to the Kings Arms pub. Head to the right of the pub along Forge Lane and into open fields. After two large fields, turn right up to a minor road.

3 Turn left and where the road ends, keep straight ahead along a track, the Pilgrims' Way. This leads on to join the North Downs Way and goes beyond the A229 through an underpass. Follow the North Downs Way along a track to a road junction.

4 From here turn left to visit the Countless Stones, then right along the North Downs Way to visit Kit's Coty. The archaeological tour over, retrace your steps to just beyond the A229.

5 Fork left off the Pilgrims' Way and take the North Downs Way up the steep scarp. As you climb, you will see the White Horse Stone a few yards to the left of the path. At the top you emerge from the woods, turn right and soon look for a short down hill path back into the woods. After a few yards turn left to follow a roughly horizontal path for ½ mile. Leave the woods to bypass the barns and buildings of Harp Farm and proceed along a minor road for about 300yds and ahead into more woodland.

6 After a level mile, arrive at a track and turn right. The track descends and bends right where the North Downs Way goes left into fields. Stay on the stony track to pass the entrance to a large chalk quarry and carry on down to a crossroads. Turn l eft here or go straight ahead, as either route will lead back into Detling.

The walk starts near the Norman church of St Martin of Tours in Detling

ALONG THE WAY

There are Stone Age relics in three places near the western edge of this walk. Kit's Coty House is the central burial chamber of a Neolithic Long Barrow, dating from about 2,000 BC. Nearby is the collection of stones, known as Countless Stones or Fallen Stones, or sometimes called Little Kit's Coty. Originally the burial chamber in a long barrow, it is now a jumbled pile of stones which are difficult to count. On the way back from these relics, the path leads past the White Horse Stone, a megalith almost hidden by vegetation in summer.

FACT FILE

Distance 10 miles
Time 4½ hours
Maps OS Landranger 188, OS Pathfinder 1193 and 1209
Start/parking Detling, on the A249 just north of Maidstone, grid ref 793582
Terrain Mostly flat, but with one steep climb up the North Downs scarp and a steep descent later
Nearest town Maidstone
Refreshments Pub and village shop in Detling and pub in Boxley
Public transport There is a bus service from Maidstone to Detling
Stiles One
Suitable for Older children

ROUND THE BATTLEFIELD

This spectacular walk includes fine views, a preserved steam railway and the site of a Civil War battleground. .

1 From the car park walk towards the town, until you pass the police station – turn right here and cut through the churchyard. At a wall bear right and follow a path all the way to the road. Bear right and cross the bridge over the railway. Passing a school and a turning to Bishop's Sutton, follow the road round to the right and when you draw level with Links Cottages, swing half-left to join the Wayfarer's Walk.

2 Follow the bridleway towards Cheriton, across the fairways of Alresford golf club. Keep a ridge of hills, topped with trees, ahead of you and beyond the fairways you enter a field. Follow the path up into the trees and then down a woodland ride to the B3046. Turn left and follow the road to the first right bend. Swing left by a cottage, still on the Wayfarer's Walk, and follow a grassy track between trees and hedgerows. Turn sharp right at a junction and go down to the road.

3 Go straight over and turn left by some cottages and barns to follow a grassy path parallel to the River Itchen. Cross several field boundaries and, when the houses of Cheriton come into sight, join a path in the field corner and follow it between the fence and hedgerow. Turn left at the lane and walk to the centre of Cheriton, then bear right at the junction and pass a private house with the letters 'HH'. Continue along the B3046, passing the entrance to Cheriton House. At a right bend, by a thatched cottage, go straight on along a track under some yew trees.

4 At some bungalows and a greenhouse turn right, down to the road. Follow it to the junction with the A272, cross it and take the road signposted to Kilmeston and Droxford. The source of the Itchen, one of Hampshire's great trout rivers, is in the fields over to the right. At a sharp right bend, by some woodland, turn left to join a muddy track. Soon you can make out the outline of Hinton Ampner House. When you reach the Wayfarer's Walk, turn left and follow the path through the parkland. Look for a white gate and a nearby cottage. Once through the gate, the Saxon church in front of you, turn right and pass through some wrought iron gates. Walk down to the road.

5 Go straight over and continue on the Wayfarer's Walk. Pass a house on the right, go over a junction of tracks and on up to the brow of the hill and down the other side to some beech trees. Turn right here and follow the path along the field edge. In the far corner go through a gate and bear left to join a track. Follow it beneath ancient beech trees. Keep on the clear track as it cuts through the undulating countryside. There is a brief stretch of road and as it bends right, go straight ahead on the next stage of the track. Follow it beside a transmitter and at a fork keep left.

6 At the next junction of tracks veer left for several yards towards the sewage treatment works, then bear right to follow a clear track through a tunnel of trees; when it emerges go straight on across Alresford golf club. There is a right of way here. Aim for a gate by the bypass, turn left and follow the embankment to the footbridge. Cross this and retrace your steps to the station car park at Alresford.

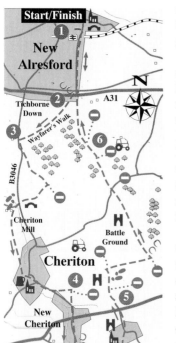

FACT FILE

Distance 8½ miles
Time 3½–4 hours
Map OS Landranger 185
Start/parking Alresford railway station car park, grid ref 587325
Terrain Field paths, tracks, some stretches of road
Nearest town Winchester
Refreshments Pubs and cafés in Alresford. The Flower Pots at Cheriton
Public transport Alresford is served by local bus services
Stiles A few
Suitable for Children, dogs and older people

ALONG THE WAY

From Alresford you can take a 10-mile steam ride along the preserved Mid Hants Watercress Line, which provided a vital link for the local watercress industry until it fell victim to the Beeching axe. For train times, tel **01962 734866**. Hinton Ampner House, a National Trust property, was expertly rebuilt in the 1960s following a fire and the garden offers a variety of delightful walks. For details of opening times, tel **01962 771305**. The return leg passes the site of an important Civil War battle. The outcome – a Parliamentary victory – halted the Royalist advance towards London.

VILLAGE GREENS

Take a pleasant walk along the trackbed of the former Hertford to Welwyn railway line, now a public footpath. You return via the pretty villages of Letty Green and East End Green, home of author Frederick Forsyth.

1 The walk starts from the car park outside Hertford Town Football Club. From here, take the path to the railway viaduct. Turn right and then left after the viaduct to reach the Cole Green Way, and follow this for 4 miles. Pass through a cutting and under a bridge before you reach the site of the former Hertingfordbury station. Beyond the station cross a road bridge. The path leads through pleasant open countryside and, further along, rises steeply to cross a road where the former bridge has been replaced. About 1 mile further on you reach the site of the former Cole Green halt, from which the footpath takes its name. There is a picnic site here and a few yards along the lane is The Cowpers Arms pub.

2 From Cole Green, walk to the end of the trackbed, turning left uphill just before the A414 road, and walk through the trees. When you arrive at the gate, turn left to follow the path leading away from the road. Walk through the trees, emerging onto a gravel drive that leads into the pretty village of Letty Green. Walk up to the crossroads and turn right into Woolmer Lane.

3 From the crossroads, walk along the lane, passing Rochford's Nurseries on your left, go past Piper's End Road and continue into East End Green. Walk past the houses and, where the track goes downhill and bends left, turn sharp right up a concrete drive (signed to Roxford ½ mile). Turn left onto a pathway through

the bushes, bearing right to pass through a broken gate and emerge onto open land. Continue next to a hedge, and then follow the path to the left, skirting the edge of a wood, before joining a track leading downhill.

4 Enjoy the views across the Lea Valley on the way down and, just before the track bends right at the bottom of the hill, turn left through a gate (signed St Mary's Lane). When the path bends right, go through another gate and walk uphill, passing Waterhall on your right. Yet another gate takes you further uphill through the trees. When you emerge on open ground, again enjoy the views across the valley to Bayfordbury College, a large white building.

5 Follow the path to the end, then turn left to walk along a lane. After a few yards you reach the former railway bridge at Hertingfordbury. If you want to stop for refreshments, continue along the lane, turning left by St Mary's Church, to emerge opposite The Prince of Wales pub.

6 Retracing your steps from the pub, pass under the bridge and turn left. Head up a gravel drive, keeping the former station house on your left, and walk parallel to the Cole Green Way. When you reach some cottages, keep straight ahead, then go through a gate, through the trees and under the railway viaduct to return to the start.

FACT FILE

Distance 9 miles
Time 4 hours
Map OS Landranger 166
Start/parking Car park by Hertford Town Football Club, grid ref 319119
Terrain Easy going, mostly well-defined paths
Nearest towns Hertford, Hatfield, Welwyn Garden City
Refreshments The White Horse, Castle Street, Hertford and The Prince of Wales in Hertingfordbury – both recommended real ale pubs. Also The Cowpers Arms in Letty

Green, next to the Cole Green Way
Stiles None
Suitable for All

ALONG THE WAY

In Hertford, the castle site dates from Saxon times, although the remains that you can see today are all Norman. The gatehouse, however, dates from 1461. St Andrew's Street contains many 17th to 19th century houses and Christ's Hospital School at the opposite end of town is late 17th century.

The Cole Green Way, the former Great Northern railway line, closed to passenger traffic between Hertford and Welwyn in 1951, but freight traffic lingered on into the 1960s.

WHERE EAGLES LAND

This breezy walk offers fine, wide views over west Hampshire. There is the added attraction of a visit to the renowned Hawk Conservancy.

1 From the Black Swan turn right and immediately right again towards Amport. Go over the Pillhill Brook, a tributary of the River Anton, and at the first bend go straight ahead, alongside Corner Cottage, towards Manor Farm. At the next gate bear left to join a waymarked path. Go through a kissing gate and walk along the edge of the field. Disregarding the next kissing gate, veer right and keep the field boundary on your immediate left. In the top corner bear right and make for the stile in the next corner, completing three sides of the field in all. On the right you get a good view of Monxton, its pretty cottages and church sheltering in the semi-wooded valley. Cross the stile and turn left, then walk along the field edge, taking in the wide views. Follow the hedge round to the right, then left. Keep to the clear path running through the fields and eventually you come to a line of trees and some houses. Bear left and follow the field boundary to the road.

2 Turn left and head for the entrance to the Hawk Conservancy. After a visit, continue along the road towards Monxton and Amport. When you reach the junction, just beyond Cob Mews, turn left for about 25yds. Turn right on to a track and then recross the Pillhill Brook at a pretty spot. Follow the track up the slope and at the road bear left for about 50yds.

3 On the right are two waymarked rights of way. Take the first one, a bridleway, by the entrance to Bryning Lodge. Follow the way between trees, hedgerows, banks of cowslips and nettles. Keep to the bridleway all the way to the road and at this point turn right, immediately passing beneath a railway line. Follow a quiet country lane; it eventually curves to the right, through a tunnel of trees. At the end of the trees you pass a private road on the right. After about 70yds bear left through a gap in a line of trees. Follow a signposted track as it swings left and follows a field edge with woodland on the left. At the end of this tunnel the track goes across an open landscape of fields and far-reaching views, with traces of woodland in the distance. When you reach some corrugated barns continue ahead on a clear, wide track.

4 Follow the track through the fields; pass a turning on the left to a bungalow and continue on the dusty track towards Abbotts Ann. When you arrive at the outskirts of the village walk down to the junction by the Old Bakery Cottage. Turn left here and head towards Monxton.

5 The road climbs gradually out of the village and from the higher ground there are good views over the surrounding Hampshire countryside. Pass the buildings of Manor Farm, recross the railway, drop down through the trees into Monxton and at the T-junction cross over to the car park where you started.

FACT FILE

Distance 6½ miles
Time 3 hours (allow longer to visit the Hawk Conservancy)
Map OS Landranger 185
Start/parking Patrons' car park at the Black Swan, Monxton (ask the landlord for permission), grid ref 314444
Terrain Easy field paths, bridleways and tracks. Some stretches of quiet road
Nearest town Andover
Refreshments The Black Swan, Monxton, the Eagle at Abbotts Ann, café at the Hawk Conservancy
Public transport Amport and District Bus Company operates a local service (No 1) from Andover, tel 01264 772307

Stiles A few
Suitable for All, but no dogs in the grounds of the Hawk Conservancy, and children under 15 must be accompanied by an adult

ALONG THE WAY

Monxton and Abbotts Ann are villages of picturesque thatched cottages and period houses. During the Second World War the Black Swan at Monxton was frequented by fighter pilots based at nearby Middle Wallop – among them, supposedly, was the legendary war hero Douglas Bader.

The Hawk Conservancy is a specialist centre for birds of prey of the world, including hawks, falcons, eagles, owls and vultures. There are daily flying demonstrations and you can even be photographed with one of these hunters perched on your hand! The Hawk Conservancy is open to the public from the beginning of March to the end of October, between 10.30am and 4pm (5pm in summer). Tel 01264 772252.

HEADING FOR THE TOP

Walk outward along paths, sometimes undefined, at the foot of the North Downs
and back across open grassland with fine sweeping views.

1 From the green, walk along Rectory Lane towards the Downs. After ¼ mile, turn right
along the path opposite Glebe Cottage. Enter the field and aim half-left to the far corner and
cross the railway. Turn right beyond, heading for the house in front of you.

2 At the road, turn right and cross the bridge. Don't turn left into Orchard Farm, but continue past The Harvesters. At the top of the gentle rise, opposite double wooden gates, cross
the stile on the left. Go across to the fencing and follow this above the lakes. At the gate
leading down to the causeway (private), bear half-left to the end of the bird-rearing enclosure
and again cross the railway. Make for the brick barn and, at the gate turn right, staying inside
the field. In the bottom corner, cross the stile and walk below the railway embankment.

3 At the end, turn right through the arch and cross the stile into the left field. Turn left up the
bank and make for the right-hand white house. At the back of the concrete parking space at
the left of this house, Harolyn, go through the gate. Walk beside the line of 12 conifers,
passing the goat's pen. Keep ahead through a nursery to reach a road by Sandells House. Turn
left and stay on this surfaced road, passing under another railway arch. Where the road turns
left carry straight on along the bridleway.

4 At the finger-post marking the junction with the North Downs Way, turn right through the
barriers and stay on this path at just above field level. Ignore any side tracks and you will soon
reach a residential road beyond the National Trust sign for the Pilgrims' Way. To shorten the
walk, follow the North Downs Way to the right up to the top of the hill, where you rejoin the
full walk at Mole Place, point 9.

5 Go up the residential road to the crest and bear half-left along the bridleway below the
Underbeeches drive. This leads to the A217, where the Yew Tree is 75yds to the right. Walk
up the main road to the end of the left pavement, and take the path ahead which climbs to the
junction with the North Downs Way beyond Rock Farm.

6 Turn left along the path to pass the masts. Within ½ mile, you come to a broad expanse of
grassland, at the start of which is a domed shelter. Carry on ahead, staying on the open grassland, and enjoy the fine views. You rejoin the North Downs Way further along and pass a
white Coal Tax post. Now bear left to reach a roadway by Swiss Cottage and turn left.

7 The shorter walk rejoins the main one in front of the gates to Mole Place. Follow the
bridleway opposite another Coal Tax post, along the laurel-lined perimeter fence. Keep ahead
to cross the track leading into Mount Hill. The bridleway narrows beyond
the drive to Buckland Heights. In
due course you lose height and
come to a T-junction; turn right.
Walk along a steep track and
then turn left up the opposite
bank. The path then descends
beside barbed-wire fencing to
rejoin the North Downs Way. At
the metal gate, head towards a
barn. Follow the track to the house,
then continue along the road past
Old Kemps Farm and over a level
crossing back to the start of the walk.

FACT FILE

Distance 8½ miles or 6 miles
for the shorter walk
Time 4 hours or 3 hours
Maps OS Landranger 187, OS
Pathfinder 1207
Start War Memorial opposite
St Mary's church, Buckland,
grid ref 222508
Terrain Level, but with an
ascent and descent of the
Downs escarpment
Nearest town Reigate
Parking In Rectory Lane
beside the green
Refreshments The Yew Tree,
on A217, open 11am–11pm,
grid ref 256517
Public transport Infrequent
Tillingbourne bus 573 from
Redhill and Reigate
Stiles About a dozen
Suitable for Children and
dogs

ALONG THE WAY

**Coal Tax posts are reminders
that the Corporation of the
City of London had the
right, up until 1890, to levy a
duty on coal brought into the
City. This duty helped to pay
for the rebuilding of several
churches damaged in the
Great Fire of 1666. After the
passing of the London Coal
and Wine Continuance Act,
1861, the area for collection
of duty was enlarged, and
over 200 posts were erected.
The inscription refers to this
Act.**

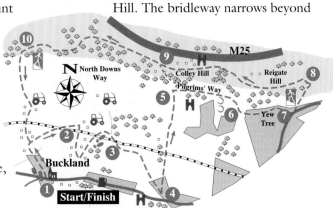

UP ON THE DOWNS

This walk from ridge top to vale gives a delightful view of the
South Downs scarp with its coombes.

1 From the car park walk east across the open grassy area,
through a gate and onto the South Downs Way path. Follow
this along the top of the scarp, where there are magnificent
views northwards over South Harting and expansive views
across the Weald, towards the sandstone hills beyond
Midhurst.

2 At the bottom of the hill is a cross-paths. Turn right here
along the South Downs Way and climb diagonally up the side
of a large dry valley. The path climbs steadily for more than ½
mile, passing through two small gates. Just before the third
gate turn sharp left along a clear track. This leads on around
the head of a magnificent dry valley down to the right, and
then uphill again. Continue over the top of Pen Hill and then
drop to a cross-paths, but keep straight ahead. Walk along the
South Downs Way round the edge of a field, through a small
wood, and then across an open field. The flint farmhouse and
large barn of Buriton Farm become visible to the right.

3 At the farm track turn left and after 20yds, where the South
Downs Way turns right, go straight ahead. When the track
begins to descend, go left through a gate and into a grassy
field, down to a stile, through a small wood, and across a field.
Cross another stile onto a track and turn right, to walk alongside a small stream.

4 At the end of this track turn left along the road, then left
again, passing several flint and chalk buildings. At the next
bend in the road, turn left again to pass through the farmyard,
between a big barn and a stone wall. Cross a stile and go
straight ahead along a field boundary, to another stile and a T-
junction of paths. Turn right here alongside a large garden
fence and then through two gates. The path leads straight
ahead alongside field margins. There are magnificent views of
the well-wooded scarp over to the left, as the footpath leads
westwards along the clay belt. After three fields the route joins
a track for a few yards. Don't bend right along this track, but
go a few yards left to continue more or less straight ahead.
Then walk alongside a wood and another field to emerge onto
a narrow road.

5 After 100yds turn left along a surfaced track, which becomes muddy beyond the house. It climbs steeply through the
wooded scarp. Emerge from the top of the woods and pass
through a gate to reach the cross-paths at point 2. Turn right
to retrace your steps to the start.

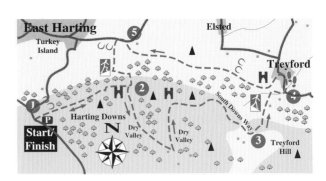

FACT FILE

Distance 8 miles
Time 4 hours
Maps OS Landranger 197, OS
Pathfinder 1285 and 1286
Start/parking Harting Down
NT car park, grid ref 792182
Terrain Some gentle climbs and
one very steep ascent of the scarp
Nearest town Petersfield
Refreshments Pubs in South
Harting

Public transport A weekday bus
service from Midhurst
Stiles Several
Suitable for Children, dogs on
leads due to sheep

ALONG THE WAY

The National Trust acquired
Harting Down in 1989. Much
of this downland area has
never been intensively farmed
and contains relics of original
grassland, traditionally grazed
by sheep. The surrounding
countryside is rich in flowers,
insects, birds and adders.
Relics of an ancient settlement
can be seen at the Iron Age
hillfort on Beacon Hill.

From the ridge top of Harting Down there are stunning views across the Weald

SOUTH WEST

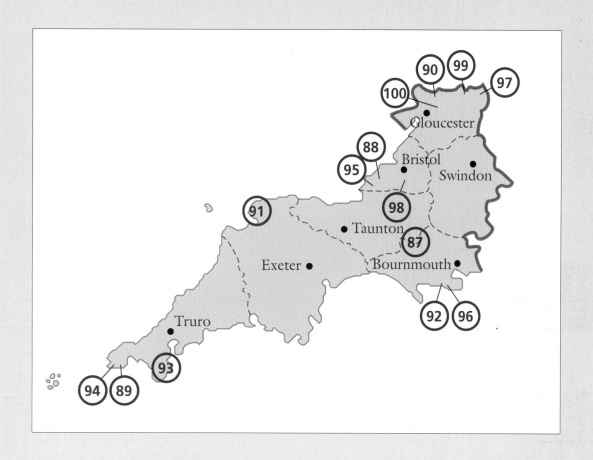

THE THRILL OF THE CHASE

This is a walk of immense contrasts. Based at the heart of the wide landscapes of Cranborne Chase, it is surprising to spend much of the route deep in woodlands or following a charming chalk stream valley.

1 From the war memorial follow the edge of the pond and turn right down a no through road. Follow this for nearly ½ mile until just before Ashmore Farm. Turn left down a clear track next to the farmhouse. This bridleway narrows after 200yds, then runs along the edge of Wiltshire Coppice. The bridleway forks about ¼ mile later. Go right, along level ground for ¾ mile, initially between a field and a hedge. Here you are on the county boundary with Wiltshire. When the field ends it is replaced by Tollard Green Wood, but the path remains clear.

2 About 50yds after the wood ends, swing right and climb, keeping the fence on your left. Reaching a track on the brow of the hill, turn right. Fork left 25yds later at a large oak, then head downhill along the edge of another wood, keeping a field on the left. At the bottom of the hill, turn left. Follow the bottom of the valley ahead. This continues through three fields, before picking up a track by a farmhouse. Follow this for ¾ mile to a minor road.

3 Turn right here and follow the road as it swings left and climbs. Turn left opposite a bungalow. Head uphill through a field, along a footpath to Tarrant Gunville. When you reach a wood, follow the path through the trees, then keep to the high ground in the next field for 30yds. Go downhill with a hedge on the right. Enter another field, swing left and head

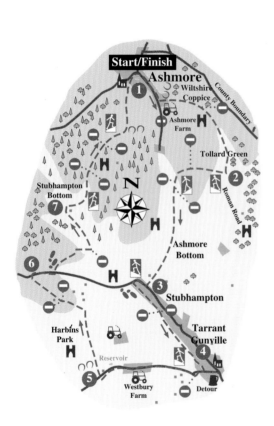

FACT FILE

Distance 11 miles
Time 5 hours
Maps OS Landranger 184 and 195
Start/parking Ashmore village, between duck pond and war memorial. Grid ref 912178
Terrain Many long, steady climbs and descents. Muddy in parts
Nearest town Shaftesbury
Refreshments Available only at the Bugle Horn in Tarrant Gunville, found on the detour to Eastbury House. Convenient half-way stop
Public transport None
Stiles A few, generally in good order
Suitable for Older children and dogs

ALONG THE WAY

At 700ft above sea level, Ashmore is Dorset's highest village. The inhabitants are proud of its pond, so when it dried out, they acted quickly to restore it. Nearly 500ft below Ashmore, Tarrant Gunville once had Dorset's largest house, Eastbury Park. A short detour takes in all that remains of a house that was too expensive for anyone to maintain.

downhill. Just before the road, turn right and follow a footpath through a field, then continue between some chicken houses to reach a track. Turn right, then in 30yds turn left and follow a level footpath through fields to emerge opposite Tarrant Gunville church. The ¼ mile detour to Eastbury House is well worth taking.

4 From the church, turn right and climb the minor road towards Everley Hill for just over 1 mile. On the brow of the hill is an underground reservoir, and 100yds beyond this you turn right.

5 Follow a clear bridleway between hedges, then along the right-hand side of Harbins Park. When this wood ends, continue ahead for 50yds, then swing left as marked. The bridleway ends ¼ mile later at a track. Continue ahead and cross a field. When you reach the narrowest part of a large wood, pass through the trees. Continue ahead through a large field, keeping woodland left, until you reach a minor road.

6 Turn right and head downhill for nearly ½ mile. Turn left at a footpath sign and follow the Wessex Ridgeway along the edge of two fields, separated by another narrow band of trees. In the left-hand corner of the second field, enter a large wood and descend steeply through the trees. At the bottom of the hill, turn left and follow a bridleway which climbs slowly. In 200yds join a wider forest track coming in from the right. Continue for ¼ mile, then turn right at a junction with another track.

7 Climb steadily for ¾ mile along this muddy bridleway. It crosses a surfaced track, then narrows, climbs again, before finally reaching a staggered junction near the end of the trees. Go virtually straight ahead, then in 100yds leave the wood and continue along a track between two fields. When this ends, turn left, follow another track for ½ mile to reach Ashmore. In the village, turn right to return to your car.

The pond in Ashmore is the pride of the village

CHEDDAR DRAMA

You will certainly need a head for heights on this walk around Cheddar Gorge. The reward is a panoramic view of the most dramatic inland rock scenery in southern England.

FACT FILE

Distance 5½ miles
Time 3½ hours
Map OS Landranger 182
Start/parking Public car park alongside the Butcher's Arms on the B3135 leading from the A371 in Cheddar Village to Cheddar Gorge. Grid ref 461535
Terrain Two steep ascents which together make 1,000ft of climbing
Nearest towns Weston-super-Mare, Wells
Refreshments Pubs and cafes in Cheddar
Public transport Cheddar is served by Badgerline Buses running from Weston to Wells
Stiles All well constructed and easy to negotiate
Suitable for Fit walkers and well-controlled dogs

ALONG THE WAY

Cheddar, with its show caves and spectacular gorge, attracts visitors from all over the country. At the end of the walk, it is worth spending an hour or two exploring both Gough's and Cox's Caves. At the head of the gorge lies the Black Roack Nature Reserve, 183 acres of rough grassland, plantation, natural woodland and scree, all sited around a dry limestone valley. Our walk follows the West Mendip Way through this valley. This 30-mile footpath runs between Weston-super-Mare and Wells.

1 Leave the car park, turn right and follow the B3135 as it makes its way up through the lower end of Cheddar Gorge. About 200yds after you pass Jacob's Ladder, you will find Rose Cottage on the left, just beyond the top end of a small reservoir. Immediately in front of Rose Cottage, turn left on to an unmetalled track. In a further 250yds, next to a driveway leading to a private residence, the footpath bears right and passes behind some more cottages. In about 100yds, at a junction, follow the path that climbs back up the hill to the right.

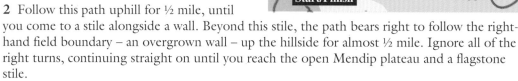

2 Follow this path uphill for ½ mile, until you come to a stile alongside a wall. Beyond this stile, the path bears right to follow the right-hand field boundary – an overgrown wall – up the hillside for almost ½ mile. Ignore all of the right turns, continuing straight on until you reach the open Mendip plateau and a flagstone stile.

3 Beyond this stile, continue ahead across three fields to reach Piney Sleight Farm, following a drystone wall on the left. The path passes to the left of the farmhouse, and beyond this you walk to the end of the farm drive. Turn right here to follow the West Mendip Way, signposted to Cheddar. This path follows the right-hand edge of two fields before entering Long Wood. Keep on the main path ahead, which descends through the trees to reach a stile leading into Black Rock Nature Reserve.

4 Follow the main path through the nature reserve, ignoring any left turns as you go, and in about ½ mile you reach the B3135. Cross this road and then follow the path opposite, signposted to Draycott. This path climbs steeply through the woods for ¼ mile where you reach a hand-gate on the hilltop.

5 About 75yds beyond this hand-gate the path forks. Ignore the signposted path to the left, which leads to Draycott. Instead keep to the right fork which takes you back to Cheddar. This path soon reaches the high ground above Cheddar Gorge. Follow the path downhill to Prospect Tower, making sure that you take a detour to the right to enjoy the spectacular view of the gorge. Follow the footpath to the left of the tower to a junction, where a right turn brings you back onto the B3135 in Cheddar. Turn left and the car park is a few yards down the road.

The rock formations around Cheddar Gorge are breathtaking

The view from the headland at Point 2

WINK FOR A DRINK

Walk to the Lamorna Wink, named because a wink at the landlord
was required to obtain a drink of contraband spirit!

1 Leave the quay car park, heading for a row of terraced cottages. Passing them on your left, cross the bridge over the stream and head uphill, following the coastal footpath sign. Continue on the rocky, well-defined footpath to the headland.

2 Walk over the top of the headland and down the other side on the wide, disguised stone steps. Follow the path along to the Kemyel Crease Nature Reserve.

3 Continue on the path through the trees and when you leave the woods turn right. The path continues along the cliffs, over two small waterfalls, and then takes a left turn, where it starts to climb gently. At the top follow the path and emerge at the bend in the minor road.

4 Walk straight ahead on the road that takes you downhill past the bird sanctuary into Mousehole. After looking around the village return to the minor road. Retrace the path until you are about 50yds past the last house on the left.

5 The footpath now continues over small farm fields separated by stiles. Climb the stile at the side of the wooden marker on the right, which has the words 'Lamorna Cove Inland Route'. Walk up the side of the field, with the hedge on your left, to the next stile on the left. Cross the stile and walk diagonally right across the field to the next stile. Over the stile, go diagonally right again. Cross the next stile and go straight ahead, with a hedge on your right, towards a farm.

6 Walk past the granite barn, keeping it to your left. Pass through the small wooden gate in front of you and go straight across the farmyard to the first wooden stile. Now continue in a straight line between the rest of the farm buildings, negotiating two more stiles.

7 Leave the farm buildings and turn left, then bear right onto a marked footpath. This becomes twisty and crosses a stream on a clapper bridge just before the next stile. Cross the stile, keeping the hedge to the right, and continue to the next stile in the corner of the field. Cross the stile onto a minor road and turn left. Pass Kemyel Crease Farm and, when the road runs out, go straight ahead to the next granite stile on the right. Over the stile, walk diagonally across the field. Cross the stile and go straight across the field, heading towards another group of farm buildings. Cross the stile, with a hedge on your right, and leave the field at the farm.

8 Continue straight ahead on a farm track to the last farm building on your right.

9 Turn left downhill, pass two overgrown quarries and rejoin the coastal path just above the cottages.

10 Turn right at the end of the cottages and walk up the valley road to the Lamorna Wink.

11 Retrace your route to the car park.

ALONG THE WAY

Earlier this century, granite from the quarry above Lamorna Cove was in great demand and was used in the building of the Embankment in London.

The conifer plantation at the Kemyel Crease Nature Reserve provides shelter for migrant birds. On the left side of the hill above Mousehole is the Wild Bird Hospital and Sanctuary. A registered charity founded in 1928, it is open daily from 10am-4pm and admission is free.

FACT FILE

Distance 6 miles
Time 2½ hours
Map OS Landranger 203
Start/parking Lamorna Cove car park, grid ref 450240
Terrain Rocky, well-defined coastal path. Fields and lanes which can be muddy after rain
Nearest town Penzance
Refreshments Lamorna Wink Inn. Seasonal café at Lamorna Cove. Numerous places in Mousehole
Public transport None

Stiles Eight granite and three wooden, all easy
Suitable for Children; dogs on leads across farmland

WALK THE WHALEBACK

Some local writers describe Bredon as a whaleback hill. If so, it's a stranded whale, cut off from the main Cotswold escarpment by glacial meltwater. Whatever you call it, you'll enjoy fine walking and great views.

1 Take a look at the church and nearby tithe barn (walk to the road and make two right turns), before walking north along Dock Lane. When it ends join a well-used, well-maintained footpath signed to Bredon's Norton. After passing through a railway tunnel bear left over a narrow field, across a road and over another field. Turn left to Bredon's Norton.

2 Turn right by a former chapel, now the village hall. After 300yds turn right on a bridleway. Pass the beautiful Manor, then turn left. Go through a small gate and skirt farm buildings and a walled garden to reach another gate. Join a good track which you can see climbing the hill. After ½ mile it levels out and swings right, soon passing the ruins of Hill Barn.

3 Reach a T-junction and turn left. The path skirts an overgrown quarry and climbs almost imperceptibly to the northern rim of the escarpment, where you turn right through a strip of woodland called The Warren. Just keep walking along the edge for 2 miles.

4 Eventually waymarks indicate the Wychavon Way. Though you don't join this it's your signal to turn right. Walk past a row of pine trees then turn right beside another row. Immediately after passing a small plantation turn left on a footpath and descend the hill, with Overbury Wood on your right for much of the way. When you join a lane continue into Overbury.

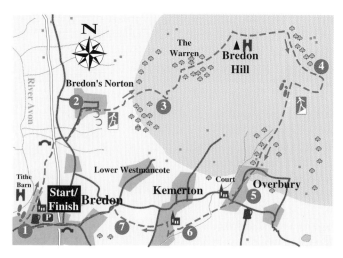

5 Turn right to see the church and Overbury Court then walk to the road. Turn left, then join an unsigned path on the right which skirts a farm. After passing a corrugated iron barn, cross a driveway to a gate and enter parkland. Go diagonally left to the far fence and climb over (dogs can slip through). Cut across the corner of a field, climb another fence, cross a stream and carry on in the same direction. After fording another stream continue to the far corner of a field where a gate gives access to a copse.

6 Turn left beside a brook, cross a footbridge and turn right towards Kemerton, passing between two ponds. Continue past a ruined watermill to a lane and turn right. Having passed the church, join the first footpath on the left. Go diagonally left across an orchard to a lane and join another footpath almost opposite. It's enclosed by hedges at first but you soon cross into the adjacent field then bear very slightly left to pass a copse.

7 Climb a stile and go straight on to reach a patch of damp woodland. Turn right on a clear path which leads to the lane at Lower Westmancote. If you've left a car in Bredon turn left. If you're catching a bus you can do so here.

FACT FILE

Distance 9½ miles
Time 4 hours
Maps OS Landranger 150, OS Pathfinders 1019 & 1042
Start St Giles Church, Bredon, grid ref 920370
Terrain Clear paths and tracks over sheep pasture, some low-lying muddy patches; gentle climb to almost 1,000ft
Nearest town Tewkesbury
Parking Car park on Dock Lane by River Avon, 200yds north of church
Refreshments Pubs and shops in Bredon and Overbury
Public transport Buses (Mon-Sat) from Tewkesbury, Evesham, Pershore and Cheltenham, tel Hereford & Worcester County Bus Line 01345 125436; Ashchurch rail station

(Tewkesbury) is likely to re-open in early 1996, tel 01452 425543 for details
Stiles About 15, one slightly awkward
Suitable for Children and dogs on leads

ALONG THE WAY

Bredon Hill is the largest of several Cotswold outliers. It has a gentle dip slope and a steep scarp and much of it is a Site of Special Scientific Interest.

Near the tower at the summit there's a rock outcrop shaped like an elephant. In the past the people of the vale climbed the hill on Good Friday to kiss the elephant, known as the Banbury Stone.
Bredon is famous for its barn. It's 132ft long and was built about 1350. It belongs to the National Trust and is open April to October on Wednesdays and Thursdays and at weekends.

The view of the River Avon and Pershore from Bredon Hill

SURF AND SAND

Avoid the crowds on a walk around this popular part of North Devon.

1 From the car park turn left and follow the road out of the village, past the lovely stone-built 12th century Church of St Mary Magdalene. On the way out of the village you pass a chapel. About 50yds further on go through a five-bar gate to reach the coast path – there is no sign here.

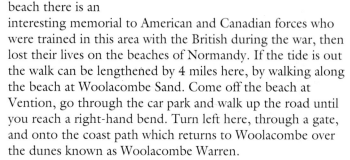

2 Turn left and walk along the coast path until it emerges onto the road. Walk down here, to just past Watersmeet Hotel, where you can walk on the grass down into Woolacombe. Above the beach there is an interesting memorial to American and Canadian forces who were trained in this area with the British during the war, then lost their lives on the beaches of Normandy. If the tide is out the walk can be lengthened by 4 miles here, by walking along the beach at Woolacombe Sand. Come off the beach at Vention, go through the car park and walk up the road until you reach a right-hand bend. Turn left here, through a gate, and onto the coast path which returns to Woolacombe over the dunes known as Woolacombe Warren.

3 Walk into Woolacombe, turn right in front of the shops and then left into the road which leads past the post office.

Follow this road past the school and go through a kissing gate. This path goes up the valley to Woolacombe Riding Stables. It turns onto a metalled lane which leads up the hill to the main road. Here turn right and then about 200yds up the hill turn left into a residential road called Woolacombe Rise. There is a track in front of you which leads uphill and eventually brings you to Poole Farm. Go onto the track and up to the main road.

4 Turn left and walk carefully along this narrow road. It is known as Mortehoe Station Road, as there used to be a station serving the village on the Barnstaple-Ilfracombe railway line. Notice the tall chimneys on the cottage at Borough Cross. Turn right at the sign to Damage Barton and go straight through the campsite. Follow the lane to Damage Barton, a grey stone 17th century farmhouse.

5 Look for a sign on a gate, signposted to Lee and Bull Point, go through the gate and follow the track. At the signpost take the track to the left to Bull Point. After 200yds cross a stile to the left. There is a small standing stone in the field, thought to be a relic from the Bronze Age. The path drops down the hill and into a deciduous valley, then carries on over a small wooden footbridge, where you turn right.

6 When you arrive at the fork in the paths take the left one which zigzags up the hill – at the top there is a lovely view down the valley to Damagehue Rock. When you reach the lighthouse path follow it down to Bull Point Lighthouse.

7 From here take the coast path south across a grassy area. The path climbs up and around some little knolls and above Rockham Bay, which is accessible from the coast path. Continue along the path until you come to a stile over a wall. Cross this and turn left, then go up the valley and back into Mortehoe. Here the path joins the road opposite North Morte Well. Walk back to the centre of the village.

FACT FILE

Distance 6½ miles or 10½ miles
Time 3 hours or 4½ hours
Map OS Landranger 180
Start Mortehoe village, grid ref 458453
Terrain Well-defined tracks and paths, some very muddy patches
Nearest town Ilfracombe
Parking Small public car park in village

Refreshments The Chichester Arms, The Ship Aground and The Smugglers Arms in Mortehoe
Public transport Devon bus operates a service from Barnstaple and Ilfracombe, tel 01392 382800
Stiles Five
Suitable for Children, dogs on leads through fields

ALONG THE WAY

The benches in Mortehoe Church feature intricate carving and it's worth a visit to have a look at them. It is sometimes possible to visit the lighthouse at Bull Point, or you can pass your time watching the surfers in the sea off this superb stretch of sand.

The long stretch of beach at Woolacombe provides an optional extra for this walk when the tide is out

PURBECK'S HIGHS AND LOWS

Kingston and Kimmeridge both boast large country houses and are only a few miles apart on the Isle of Purbeck. However, the hilltop village of Kingston is quite different to Kimmeridge, which nestles in a hollow close to the sea.

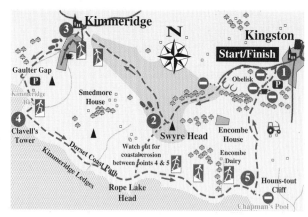

1 From the car park entrance turn left and follow the minor road for ½ mile to a parking area with information boards. Turn left here, pass between two stone pillars, then continue straight ahead to follow a clear bridleway to 'Swyre Head 1'. Swing right through the first field to pass into another, now with a wood immediately right. On the left Encombe House stands out in its own valley with man-made lakes. Carry on along the high ground and eventually swing left to climb the clear, small hummock that makes Swyre Head the highest point in Purbeck. From the top you can take in Encombe House, Smedmore House, the coast and much of the Isle of Purbeck.

2 From Swyre Head, pass left of the triangulation point and follow the bridleway to Kimmeridge. For the next 1½ miles keep a mixture of fence, wall and hedge to the left and follow the ridge with the sea on the left. The descent steepens just before a minor road, where you turn left. At a T-junction about 50yds on, go straight ahead and follow the signposted footpath to 'Kimmeridge ¼'. The descent takes you immediately left of St Nicholas' Church into the village.

3 Passing the café and post office on the left, turn right immediately after you pass the last cottage on the right. Take the marked footpath across a field and leave via a double stile and bridge. Over the bridge turn left and follow the hedge left through three fields. At the minor road go left, passing some toilets to reach a large parking area. Turn right, cross the grass and aim for the low cliff-top, which you follow towards the nature reserve centre and huts on the shoreline. Above this are the ruins of the 175-year-old Clavell's Tower. At the end of the first car park, pass through some scrub to a second grassy area, then turn right 50yds later and descend carefully to the quay and information centre. When you reach the minor road cross it and follow the signposted coast path route to climb steeply to Clavell's Tower.

4 Continue east along the coast path, watching out for landslips and steep drops, often made worse after heavy rain. This 3-mile, undulating section of the coast path enjoys views over the Kimmeridge Ledges and Swyre Head. The final 400ft climb of Houns-tout is very difficult but it is immensely rewarding.

5 At Houns-tout turn left and follow the ridge inland for about 1 mile. Pass through several fields, keeping a wall on the right and Encombe House on the left. Watch out for an obelisk, dating from 1835, just before you enter some trees. About 200yds along a track through the trees pass the Nursery Tea Rooms, then take care at a staggered junction. Keep going generally straight ahead, watching out for 'private' signs as you go, and pick up the clear footpath to Kingston. Follow this until just before the minor road, where you turn left through a small gap in the hedge to the car park.

The view down towards the sea from Swyre Head

THE FRENCH CONNECTION

Follow a stretch of the Helford River to Frenchman's Creek, then inland through woodland to the village of St Anthony-in-Meneage.

1 Turn right into Helford, crossing the wooden footbridge. Follow the street to the Shipwright's Arms, bear left to a gate marked private, then turn sharp left to follow a footpath for about 120yds. Turn right on a public footpath, go through an iron gate and continue down the National Trust footpath to Penarvon Cove, where there is a sign to Frenchman's Creek.

2 Leave Penarvon Cove by the metalled road, bearing left up a steep hill. Turn right at the top and follow the path across the field. Bear left at the next junction and walk downhill to a gate, again marked private. Turn sharp left, down a series of steps, and through a kissing gate to follow the National Trust permissive path.

3 At the next T–junction turn right to see the remains of Old Quay, then retrace your steps.

4 Continue along the path and turn left onto a concrete road leading uphill to the main road. Cross the road, go through the farmyard and into the first field, taking an ill-defined public footpath towards the woods. Carefully cross the stile to go through a wet glade. Cross a stream and turn right along the path that leads uphill. Cross another stile and follow the stoned path into a steeply sloping field.

5 Walk up this field, bearing right towards two trees which mark the stile onto the main road. Cross this and take the footpath to the right. Walk along the field hedge to a cattle grid stile and a path into Minster Meadow and Manaccan. Walk downhill past the school; the church is on the left and the New Inn to the right.

5A For the shorter route retrace your steps uphill, turn left into Minster Meadow, then follow the footpath by the field hedge to the main road. Cross the road and almost immediately turn right. Walk to the bottom left-hand corner of the field to rejoin the woodland path. At the first junction ignore the left turning which you came up earlier and continue straight along the path – this becomes a steep concrete road into Helford. Turn right over the wooden bridge and head uphill to the car park.

6 The longer route leaves Manaccan by a public footpath that turns right off the metalled road to the east of the church. In about 120yds turn right on a public footpath signed to Carne and follow the path over stiles across a series of fields to turn left onto a metalled road.

7 In a few yards a signpost to the left indicates that St Anthony is 1 mile away. Follow this road along the banks of Gillan Creek to reach St Anthony.

8 Continue up the hill behind the church for about 100yds. Look for a large house set back from the road on your right. Turn right into the drive but bear left past the house to an obvious path leading to a series of fields.

9 With the estuary on your right follow the field hedge, looking out for a stile on your right. In 75yds go through an iron kissing gate to follow a narrow undulating path, which can be very muddy, along The Gew.

10 A number of delightful coves come into view. Passing the first of these, follow the yellow arrow marking the coast path to the right, then at a fork bear left.

11 The coast path continues to an iron gate leading to a driveway and a metalled roadway. Turn right down the hill and, at the approach to Treath Cottage, turn sharp left and follow the footpath up some steps. Go through another iron gate and past the Helford Sailing Club, then turn right through a gap in the hedge to the car park.

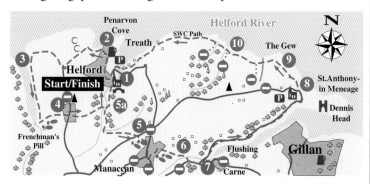

Pass delightful Gillan Creek at point 7, on the way to St Anthony

ALONG THE WAY

Frenchman's Creek is one of the chief delights of this walk. The creek, river and sea views are magnificent and the churches at Manaccan and St Anthony are worth visiting. At the former, a fig tree growing out of the church wall is said to bring bad luck to anyone who destroys so much as a leaf.

FACT FILE

Distance 8½ miles or 5½ miles
Time 5 or 3 hours
Map OS Landranger 204
Start/parking Helford village car park (fee), grid ref 760259
Terrain Undulating with some steep slopes which can be very muddy
Nearest town Helston
Refreshments The Shipwrights Arms in Helford and the New Inn in Manaccan provide excellent food and facilities all year round

Public transport Truronian Coaches operates a once-daily service on Monday, Thursday and Saturday, but the times are not convenient for walkers. Tel 01872 73453
Stiles Several, some difficult, plus some kissing gates
Suitable for Older children and well-controlled dogs on the shorter walk

CLIFFTOP THEATRE

Although the Minack open-air theatre operates only in summer, you can enjoy the spectactular backdrop of the sea all year round when walking along these cliffs.

1 Turn right out of the car park and head up the tarmac road (signed – 'no unauthorised vehicles') to Gwennap Head Coastguard Station.

2 Turn left at the Coastguard Station and walk along the cliff top path, heading back towards Porthgwarra.

3 When you reach the hamlet walk around the back of the beach slipway and the route, which is now signed as a coastal path, continues up between the cottages.

4 Take care over this next section – near the top, three granite boulders lying end to end block the path. Don't attempt to skirt around them to the right as this is very near the cliff edge – climb up them instead. The path continues along the cliff and then descends steeply passing St Levan's Well and a sandy beach below.

5 At Rospletha Cliffs, where there is a National Trust sign, walk out to the headland for the view, then return to the path, turn right and continue towards the Minack Theatre.

6 Walk straight through the theatre car park and take the path to the left of the entrance to the theatre. Here there is an alternative route signed to avoid the steep descent, however, the alternative route is also steep. Descend and follow the path to the back of the beach.

7 Continue straight across the track and head down to the beach, passing a granite waymarker that directs you towards Penberth. Walk up the cliff to the wooden gate and turn right. In about 200yds you pass two wartime look-out buildings then, in about 100yds, the track divides. Take the right fork, passing the stone pyramid, a National Trust structure with a commemorative plaque. Continue until the path divides again and take the right fork from Treen Cliffs.

8 When you join the main track from Treen village, turn right onto the headland and walk to Logan Rock.

9 From the rock retrace your steps to point 8, turn right to continue along the path and descend to Penberth Cove. For the return route, head back to point 8 then continue along the wide track straight in front, which comes out at the wooden gate above Porthcurno. Continue along the path, but without going out onto the headlands, making the return slightly shorter.

FACT FILE

Distance 8 miles
Time 4 hours
Map OS Landranger 203
Start/parking Porthgwarra car park, grid ref 370219
Terrain Rocky, well-defined coastal path. Some steep ascents and descents. No stiles
Nearest town Penzance
Refreshments None in winter
Public transport None
Not suitable for Young children or the elderly. A warning sign directs the less able to a different route behind the Minack Theatre, but this alternative route is still very steep

ALONG THE WAY

From Gwennap Head you can see Longships and Wolf Rock Lighthouses. St Levan's Well has existed since pagan times and the water is still used for baptisms. Porthcurno is the departure point for the transatlantic communications cable. The open-air Minack Theatre (open May-September) is set amid the cliffs to the west of the village, while to the east is the 60 ton rocking stone of Logan Rock. This used to move when touched until in 1824 a young naval officer dislodged it with crow bars. The Admiralty forced him to restore it but unfortunately it has lost the sensitivity of balance.

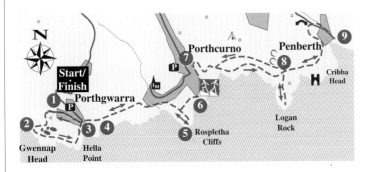

ON THE LEVEL

Explore the Somerset Levels, part of Britain's unique lowland bog. The network of drainage channels, known as rhynes are all that prevent the landscape from reverting to primeval marsh.

1 Head out of Wedmore on the B3139 Burnham road which runs alongside the village church. Follow it for ½ mile, until you arrive opposite Wedmore County First School, where you turn left onto a quiet lane. In 100yds, turn right at a junction and, almost immediately, left onto a shady, enclosed bridlepath. This secluded, occasionally muddy, path heads south for ½ mile to another lane.

2 Turn right and, in 100yds, follow the signposted bridleway on the left-hand side. This runs for ¼ mile as an enclosed green lane to a gate. Beyond it the bridleway continues as a gravelled lane past a couple of isolated cottages into the village of Heath House. There are magnificent views of the Levels.

3 At Heath House, turn left at the road junction and follow the lane down onto Tealham Moor – ignore an early cul-de-sac on the right. 150yds beyond the bridge across Old Rhyne, turn left onto a drove track that heads across Aller Moor. Follow this drove for over 1½ miles to the B3151 Westhay to Wedmore road, going straight across at one prominent cross-track the way.

4 Cross the B3151 and follow the minor road opposite that heads across the northern edge of Westhay Moor. In ½ mile, opposite an old nursery building, turn right onto a track. Follow this south for just over 1 mile to a lane, turn left and continue for 1 mile until you reach another one on the left-hand side. Follow this northwards, back across Westhay Moor, passing the flooded peat workings that now form Greater Westhay Reserve.

5 When the track reaches the road, turn right and continue for ½ mile to a junction. A left turn takes you steeply up past Batch Farm to the hilltop and a road junction. Turn right and, in 150yds, go left onto a lane that winds its way downhill into Theale and the B3139. Turn left and continue along the B3139 for 150yds before taking the first lane on the right. This passes Yew Tree Farm and North Corner Farm before heading out towards Yeo Moor.

6 A hundred yards past Yeo Moor Rhyne, the road bears right. At this point, continue ahead along a cul-de-sac lane that ends by a group of farm buildings. Continue along the track beyond these buildings to the River Axe. Cross the river and turn left, following the north bank of the Axe for 1½ miles.

7 Ignore the first footbridge across the water and continue for another ¼ mile until you reach an ornate iron bridge. Once over the river, cross the gate on the left-hand side. Almost immediately, turn right into an open field. Follow the right-hand side of this field to a footbridge across a rhyne in the top corner. Cross towards the top right-hand corner of the next field and another footbridge across yet another rhyne. In a third field, cross to the gateway opposite, beyond which a track continues for 1 mile back into Wedmore.

FACT FILE

Distance 12 miles
Time 4–5 hours
Map OS Landranger 182
Start Wedmore parish church, grid ref 435479
Terrain The steep hill that separates Westhay Moor from Yeo Moor interrupts an otherwise horizontal landscape
Nearest towns Wells and Axbridge
Parking On the B3139 alongside the church

Refreshments The George in Wedmore is next to the church
Public transport Buses from Burnham-on-Sea to Wells pass through Wedmore, except on Sundays
Stiles Almost non-existent on the Levels where drainage channels, or rhynes, and narrow footbridges separate the fields
Suitable for Well-behaved dogs

ALONG THE WAY

It was at Wedmore that King Alfred signed the historic treaty which finally severed the Danish hold on southern England. Nowadays, the many Georgian properties in the village attract commuters and retired well-to-do citizens.

The exhausted peat workings on Westhay Moor now form the Greater Westhay Reserve. The River Axe flows out from beneath the Mendips at Wookey Hole to the Bristol Channel south of Weston-super-Mare. North of Wedmore, the river drains much of Yeo Moor.

A DIFFERENT PERSPECTIVE

Corfe Castle is probably Dorset's most famous landmark but this walk approaches it differently. Take your camera and snap this postcard favourite from some unusual angles.

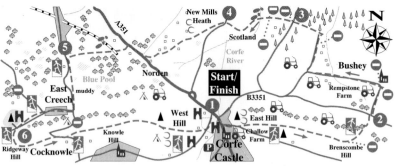

1 From the car park, turn left towards the village. When the road bends right 200yds later, head up Sandy Hill Lane under the railway bridge. About 20yds after Challow car park, turn left and follow the bridleway signposted to Ulwell. After 150yds, fork left to Rollington Hill and climb steadily to a radio station. Pause to admire the views, then continue uphill through a gate with a fence on your left. Follow this as it swings left and heads downhill, then pick up a track which passes through old coppice woodland and ends at the B3351.

2 Cross the road and head towards Rempstone. At the junction ¼ mile or so later, swing left and continue for another mile through Bushey to a T-junction, where you turn right. After ½ mile leave the road and go straight ahead along the marked bridleway for almost ½ mile, to another T-junction.

3 Cross this road and take the footpath along the edge of the wood, ignoring the bridleway to Hartland Moor. When this wide path eventually swings right, continue straight ahead down a narrow path to a road. Cross this, go over a cattle grid and ditch, then continue diagonally left for 30yds to a small gate in a raised hedge opposite. A bridge takes you over the Corfe River, then go diagonally left again across a narrow field. Cross another bridge, head diagonally left to a gateway, then diagonally right in the next field to another gate. Follow the footpath arrow up to the brow of the hill, then walk along a single file path through the centre of the field. Towards the end it widens, swings right and enters the rear of the farmyard at Scotland. Turn left to join a track leading to a minor road.

4 Turn left at the road, continue for 200yds, then follow the bridleway to Norden. This dead-straight track only bends to left and right at New Line Farm. When it reaches the A351, turn right for 400yds, then cross carefully towards Motala Kennels. In 75yds fork right, swing to the right of a farm, then continue along a grassy path and over an old railway line. The path on the other side is narrow, passes through heathland and eventually runs beside the fence around Blue Pool. Continue ahead along the edge of the Blue Pool car park and up its entry road to a minor road.

5 Turn left and head uphill for 100yds. As the road swings right, leave it and take a clear but muddy footpath straight ahead – this climbs to return to the minor road. Continue uphill, then fork right to the lovely hamlet of East Creech. Beyond this, fork left and head uphill to the layby at the base of Creech Barrow. Turn left here and climb the footpath to Ridgeway Hill.

6 At the top, turn left and follow the byway signposted to Corfe along the Purbeck Ridge. The sea is visible on three sides: to the right at Clavel's Tower, ahead in Swanage Bay and to the left in Poole Harbour. When you reach a minor road follow it for 50yds, then continue along the ridge path to Corfe. At Mary Baxter's stone, keep on towards Corfe, through a succession of fields, heading downhill. Join a bridleway coming from the right on lower ground, then follow this to a minor road. Turn left and follow it back to the car park.

FACT FILE

Distance 11 miles
Time 5 hours
Map OS Landranger 195
Start Corfe Castle village, grid ref 958825
Terrain Two quite tough climbs, but long, level sections too. Route well marked. Path between Wytch and Scotland less obvious

Nearest town - Wareham
Parking National Trust car park at base of Corfe Castle (fee)
Refreshments Café in car park and many food stops in the village
Public transport Daily service passes through Corfe Castle between Swanage and Wareham
Stiles A few
Suitable for Older children and dogs

ALONG THE WAY

The hill-top walking either side of Corfe Castle is rewarding, but short detours to Blue Pool and Creech Barrow will bring the most out of the route. The castle, owned by the National Trust, was destroyed by the Roundheads in the Civil War. From March to end October it is open from 10–5.30 (or dusk if earlier). From November to February it is open on Saturdays and Sundays only, from 12–3.30pm.

Corfe Castle is one of the most impressive ruins in England

GLORIOUS GARDENS

This upland walk, with glorious views, visits two of Britain's finest gardens at Hidcote Manor and Kiftsgate Court.

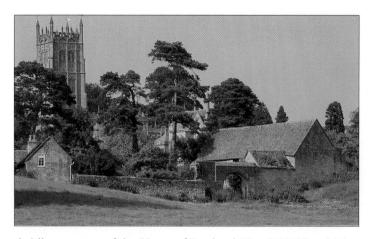

The lovely tower of St James's church at nearby Chipping Camden

1 From Mickleton church join a bridleway, part of the Heart of England Way (HEW), which skirts the churchyard. Fork right across a meadow to a small gate, after which the route is obvious. When the HEW turns right, stay on the waymarked bridleway. Go through a gateway, then climb to the entrance to Kiftsgate Court, where you'll find a gate to the lane. Follow the signs to Hidcote.

2 You soon reach the car park. Turn right to see the Manor and Hidcote Bartrim. Return to the car park and join a bridleway which goes straight uphill. When it forks go to the right, continuing towards three radio-telephone masts on top of Ebrington Hill. Cross a lane, entering Warwickshire, and continue straight on, heading for two more masts. Pass through a small copse, keeping left of a large oak tree and go through a hunting gate to a lane. Cross to the track opposite, which leads past the two masts.

3 In about ½ mile you'll see Ilmington down to the left. After a few yards you reach a junction. Turn right downhill then right again on joining a surfaced bridleway. Walk towards Foxcote mansion and turn right past it.

4 At Foxcote Farm turn right on another bridleway which climbs gently. Look for a junction beyond an uncultivated patch. Turn left, keeping to the right of a hedge until it turns a corner near a shack. Head across the field, bearing left to a gate in the corner. Follow a farm track to a lane and turn right.

5 At a junction go through two gates on the left and follow a footpath downhill. Keep left of a stone wall, then bear left over hummocky ground onto a farm track to Hidcote Boyce. Walk through the village to a T-junction and join a waymarked footpath opposite. This leads to a barn where you can join HEW. Follow this route into Mickleton.

FACT FILE

Distance 8 miles
Time 3½ hours
Maps OS Landranger 151, OS Pathfinder 1020
Start/parking Park at Hidcote if you're visiting the garden, grid ref 177429; or park in Mickleton, grid ref 161435; the directions below start at Mickleton
Terrain Undulating; good paths; arable, pasture and woodland
Nearest town Chipping Campden
Refreshments National Trust café at Hidcote; Three Ways Hotel and Butcher's Arms in Mickleton, shop in Mickleton (closed Sundays)
Public transport Sundays and Bank Holiday Mondays May to end of September Cotswold Connection 166 links Worcester, Tewkesbury and Stratford via the Vale of Evesham and northern Cotswolds, calling at Mickleton; there are rather sparse buses from Stratford, Evesham, Cheltenham and Oxford – tel 01345 125436 or 01452 425543
Stiles Several, easy
Suitable for Children; no dogs in the gardens

ALONG THE WAY

Kiftsgate Court garden is famous for its rare shrubs, and is open April until late September; Wednesday, Thursday and Sunday afternoons, also Saturdays and Bank Holiday Mondays in June and July.

IMPRESSIVE AQUEDUCTS

The first spadeful of soil was lifted in the name of the Kennet and Avon Canal in 1794. This towpath trail, centred on the beautiful Limpley Stoke Valley passes the canal's two most impressive aqueducts.

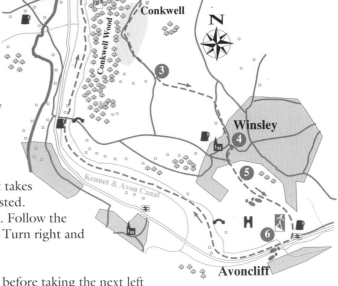

1 From the crane by the wharf, cross the canal using the footbridge on your left. Cross the aqueduct, and at the end of the path climb the stile into Conkwell Woods. You could now head straight uphill on the bed of an old mineral tramway, but our route bears left into an open field. Head diagonally across it, taking in the open views of the Avon Valley, until you reach a stile. Climb this and follow the path uphill, alongside the woodland, into Conkwell.

2 The first cottage on your right is called Spring Cottage. Bear right immediately past it, onto a waymarked path. Follow this through woodland for about ½ mile, before joining a quiet country lane. Turn right along this lane and follow it for ½ mile through open countryside. On a clear day, you should be able to make out the Marlborough Downs away to the east.

3 At a bend in the road, near Conkwell Grange, a stile on your left takes you into open fields. The right of way is, unfortunately, not signposted. Cross the first field, aiming to the right of the clump of trees ahead. Follow the right-hand boundary of the second field out onto the lane beyond. Turn right and head towards Church Farm and Winsley.

4 When you reach the Winsley bypass, cross over into Late Broads before taking the next left into Millbourne Close. Follow the footpath on the right that leads up to St Nicholas church, in the centre of the village. Continue along the lane in front of the church to the B3108. Turn right and, just beyond the Seven Stars, bear left along the lane signed to the village hall and the bowling club. Continue along this lane to a stile a short distance past the village cricket club.

5 Follow the enclosed path down the hillside beyond this stile, avoiding a right fork. Halfway down the hillside, the path passes through a kissing gate. Cross the track ahead, and take the public right of way diagonally across the open field ahead, continuing downhill into Avoncliff.

6 From Avoncliff, the 2-mile return journey to Dundas follows the canal towpath. Make sure that you take the waymarked route to Limpley Stoke – walk along the path under Avoncliff Aqueduct to reach the opposite towpath.

FACT FILE

Distance - 5 miles
Time 3 hours
Maps OS Landrangers 172 & 173
Start Dundas Wharf, 4 miles south of Bath beside the A36 Warminster road, grid ref 784626
Terrain A steep ascent and a steep descent interrupt what is otherwise a level excursion
Nearest town Bath
Parking Layby on the A36 above Dundas Aqueduct at the start

Refreshments The Seven Stars in Winsley and the Cross Guns at Avoncliff are both on the route
Public transport Bath to Bradford-on-Avon buses pass the start of the walk
Stiles A handful of easily negotiated stiles
Suitable for Active children and well-controlled dogs

ALONG THE WAY

At Dundas and Avoncliff lie the Kennet and Avon Canal's two most impressive aqueducts. Dundas Wharf also marks its junction with the Somerset Coal Canal. The hillsides above the Kennet and Avon were quarried for their golden limestone, used extensively in the building of Georgian Bath. The tiny hamlet of Conkwell, now a rural hideaway for commuters, once provided homes for the local quarry workers. This walk is in the beautiful Limpley Stoke Valley which carries the River Avon from Bath through to Bradford-on-Avon.

WAYS TO WINCHCOMBE

Unspoilt Winchcombe, where the Cotswold Way, Wychavon Way, Wardens' Way and Windrush Way meet, is a perfect base for exploring the northern Cotswolds

1 Follow the Wardens' Way along Vineyard Street towards Sudeley Castle. When you reach a cattle grid turn right into pastureland. Keep close to the fence until it turns a corner, then carry straight on until you reach a dead tree. From here, aim for a tall poplar in the left corner. There's a stile hidden nearby, and from this point on the Wardens' Way is clearly waymarked, using a yellow arrow with the addition of a green W on a white spot. Look out for these and you're unlikely to go wrong.

2 When you reach Parks Farm take care not to miss the left turn. The path is climbing now and if you look back there are excellent views.

3 The route is mostly simple, heading straight through Guiting Wood but there is one junction where the waymarked post has fallen over – it's straight on here, along the woodland edge. The path emerges into pasture by a stone lodge and you go straight on to Guiting Power.

4 At the junction near the village school it's time to leave the Wardens' Way. Turn right along the lane for ¾ mile, then go left. Just before you reach a stream you'll see two adjacent gates. Go through the left-hand one and walk through a field, with a pond on your right. At the far side of the field there are two signs for the Windrush Way, which is waymarked with a green semi-circle. Our route lies to the right.

5 At Hawling Lodge Farm here's a choice of routes and a chance for further exploration. Areas of flower-rich grassland are open to the public under the Countryside Stewardship Scheme, and three permissive paths have been waymarked. These link up with the Windrush Way. There's a good map on the site, so only the Windrush Way is shown on our map.

6 Soon, after going right at Roel Gate crossroads, you turn left. The signpost is incorrectly aligned here, so be careful. The right of way is along the surfaced track. After this the Windrush Way leads to Waterhatch Farm and through the valley of Beesmoor Brook to rejoin your outward route near Sudeley Castle.

FACT FILE

Distance 13½ miles
Time 6 hours
Maps OS Landranger 163, OS Pathfinder 1067
Start/parking The Square, Winchcombe, grid ref 024282
Terrain Undulating, good paths, muddy patches in Guiting Wood
Nearest town Winchcombe
Refreshments In Winchcombe The Old Corner Cupboard Inn is universally recommended, while The Plaisterers Arms and Lady Jane's Tea Room both specifically welcome walkers; in Guiting Power there's a shop and a pub
Public transport Monday to Saturday daytime services from Cheltenham and Broadway operated by Castleways Coaches, tel 01242 602949; evening and Sunday services provided by Marchant's Coaches, tel 01242 522714; connect with trains at Cheltenham, and with National Express at Cheltenham and Broadway
Stiles A few, none of them difficult
Suitable for Energetic children, well-controlled dogs

Map labels: Start/Finish Winchcombe (1), (2), (3) Guiting Wood, (4), (5), (6), N, Guiting Power, Nature Reserve, Access land under Countryside Stewardship Scheme, Hawling

Location map labels: Great Malvern, Evesham, WARWICK, Tewkesbury, Cheltenham, Gloucester, GLOUCESTER, Wood, Witney, Stroud, Cirencester, Nailsworth, Malmesbury, Wantage

ALONG THE WAY

Winchcombe once had a royal palace and an abbey, and was capital of a shire which was absorbed into Gloucestershire in the 11th century. Today it's a rewarding place to explore, its long streets lined with lovely cottages. Much of Sudeley Castle dates from the 15th century. Henry VIII was a frequent visitor, and his widow Katherine Parr lived here after his death.

The Wardens' Way and Windrush Way were devised by the Cotswold Voluntary Wardens. Each walk is about 13 miles long and uses a different route to link Winchcombe with Bourton-on-the-Water. A booklet about the walks is available from Winchcombe tourist information office, tel 01242 602925. Guiting Power is a lovely village. There's a Gloucestershire Wildlife Trust reserve beyond the church on the Wardens' Way which is open to Trust members, tel 01453 822761.

There are superb views from Sudeley Hill, on the Warden's Way

HIDDEN GEMS

Discover two virtually unknown villages in the Coln Valley on
this lovely walk through peaceful countryside.

Enjoy the peace of the countryside between Brockhampton and Sevenhampton

FACT FILE

Distance 6 miles
Time 2½ hours
Maps OS Landranger 163, OS
Pathfinder 1067
Start Whittington turn on
A40, grid ref 013205
Terrain Pasture, arable and
woodland with gentle gradients
and good paths
Nearest town Cheltenham
Parking Small layby on A40
opposite the Whittington turn,
also a larger one a little to the
west (if using this one take
signed path to Whittington to
avoid walking along A40)
Refreshments The Craven
Arms at Brockhampton
Public transport On
Mondays to Saturdays there are
numerous buses from
Cheltenham, Moreton and
Stow, also several from
Gloucester, Tewkesbury and
Oxford; on Sundays your best
bet is the Gloucester/
Cheltenham to Oxford route;
tel Pulhams on 01451 820369,
Swanbrook on 01242 574444
or the County Council on
01452 425543
Stiles A few, including one
ladder-type
Suitable for Children and
dogs

ALONG THE WAY

The River Coln rises below
Cleeve Hill and joins the
Thames at Lechlade. There
are several lovely villages
along its course but only
Bibury and Arlington are
well known.

Brockhampton Park, now
divided into flats, was built
in 1639 for the Craven
family, associated with the
town of Craven Arms in
Shropshire. In
Brockhampton what looks
like an ordinary farmhouse
next to the pub is the old
brewery. Opposite it is a
cottage with an unusual
sundial on its wall.

As you cross the final field
you'll notice the humps and
holloways of the deserted
medieval village of
Whittington. The site of a
Roman villa has been
discovered in the same field.

1 Walk along the lane into Whittington, passing the tiny
church and the 16th century Court. Turn left at a T-junction
and shortly fork right on a no through road which becomes a
bridleway. This leads through woodland and past disused
quarries, now reclaimed by nature and full of flowers in
season. On leaving the wood the bridleway passes more
former quarries, then contours round the base of a twin-
domed hill before skirting more woodland.

2 At a T-junction turn right into the wood and once you've
passed through it keep going to reach a junction with a
footpath. Turn left on an obvious track.

3 Turn right along a lane then take the first left, Park Lane,
enjoying excellent views now that you have reached a height
of 860ft. Go straight on at a crossroads, passing the imposing
mansion of Brockhampton Park and you soon enter the
village.

4 Turn right along a no through road to the Craven Arms
and join a footpath signed to Sevenhampton. Fully
waymarked, it passes through the Coln Valley to emerge in St
Andrew's churchyard at Sevenhampton. Leave the churchyard
by the main gate and join a footpath opposite which leads to
Lower Sevenhampton. Here you cross the Coln then follow it
to a lane. Cross the river again by a footbridge next to a ford,
then walk up the lane to a road.

5 Join a footpath opposite which goes straight ahead along
field-edges. When you reach a damaged section in the wall on
your right bear left across two fields to a lane.

6 There are two footpaths
opposite. Take the left-
hand one, going
diagonally across
two fields, then
down the right-
hand edge of
another. Turn
left to a lane.
Cross to a
footpath opposite
and walk round the
right-hand edge of a field
to reach another. The path
goes more or less straight across
to Whittington.

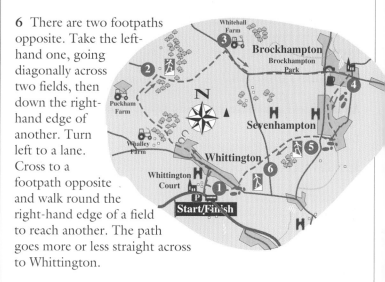

LIST OF CONTRIBUTORS

Maps by Jeremy Ashcroft

Trevor Anthill (West Midlands): Shakespeare Country; Thatches and Wells; Edge of the Wilderness

Brian Beadle (Yorkshire): Cold Comfort; Clifftops and Caves; Moorland Memorial; Beauty and Misery

Paul Biggs (East Midlands): Ancient and Modern; Roman Round; Castle Country; Taste of the Midshires; Home of the Plotters

Nick Channer (South East): Line of Defence; Smuggler Country; Round the Battlefield; Where Eagles Land

Martin Collins (Wales): Crowning Glories; Peaks of Perfection

Guy Corbett-Marshall (South West): The Thrill of the Chase; Purbeck's Highs and Lows; A Different Perspective

Paddy Dillon (Ireland and the North): Scale Force in Style; Black and White; The Long Valley; Poet's Favourite; Cork's Hills and Plains; Hill of the Fairy Calves; Bouldery Blue Stacks

John Fenna (Wales): Quiet Waterway

Jack French (East Anglia): Holding the Fort; Camping Ground; Down by the Riverside

Claire Gibbons (South West): Surf and Sand

John Gillham (North West): Secrets Revealed; Bowland's Best Crags

Colin Hogarth (Scotland): Mighty Morrone; Sand and Scots Pine; Thundering Waters; Along the Rugged Edge; Round the Little Loch

Brian Holman (East Midlands): Red Hill Contrasts

Peter Jackson (Scotland): Reach for the Heights

Nick Jenkins (Wales): Peaceful Waters; Gentle Giants

Andrew Lambert (Yorkshire): Forest and Fell; Desolate Beauty

Liz Lea (Scotland): Natural Paradise

Malcolm McKenzie (East Midlands): Way to a Windmill

Margaret McManners (North): Magnificent Moorland; Land of Singing Waters; Woods in the Ware; A Fertile Plain

David McVey (Scotland): Rob Roy Territory

Laurence Main (Wales): Bandit Country; The Fossil Forest; Views from Fron Goch; Tregaron's Nature Trail

Julie Meech (South West and West Midlands): Lore and Legend; Wild Wyre; Where Buzzards Fly; On Benthall Edge; Land of the Marcher Lords; Woodland Trek; Walk the Whaleback; Hidden Gems; Ways to Winchcombe; Glorious Gardens

Carole Nadin (East Anglia): Winding Waterways; Buried Treasure; Ships and Swans;

Dennis Needham (North West): On the Waterfront

Mick Payne (South East): House Beautiful; Doves and Ducks

Anthony Pepper (Yorkshire): Call of the Wild; Ancient Civilisations

Ivan Rabey (South West): The French Connection

Clive Scott (South East): The Forgotten Well; Heading for the Top

Jason Smalley (North West): Sandstone Stroll; Limestone Landscape

Derek Spiers (East Midlands): Estate Secrets; Peak Performance; Making Tracks; Shivering Mountain

Arnold Underwood (Yorkshire): The Forgotten Village

Nigel Vile (South West): Cheddar Drama; On the Level; Impressive Aqueducts

Maggie Weston (South West): Wink for a Drink; Clifftop Theatre

Robert Wilson (South East): Mausoleum and Manor; Ridges and Beechwoods

Philip Wood (South East and East Anglia): Picture Postcards; Round the Manor; Village Greens

Roy Woodcock (South East): Up on the Downs; Seven to One; Good Sports; Safe Haven; Ancient and Modern

Further photographs contributed by:

Alan Bedding: page 87
David Broadbent: page 79
John Buttress: page 14
Paul Felix: page 137
Fowkes/David Broadbent Photography: page 61
Sheila French: page 93
Gordon Gadsby: page 54
John Gillham: page 46
Jim Henderson: page 15

Brian Hibbert: page 8
David Lea: page 18
Julie Meech: page 72
Pembrokeshire Coast National Park: page 101
Kev Reynolds: page 121
Jason Smalley: page 48
Ian Strachan: page 10
Ian West: page 132
Ron Westlake: page 143
Jeremy Weston: page 138
Jim Winkley: page 94
Philip Wood: page 112

INDEX OF PLACE NAMES